Be sure to visit the Build The New City Website at
www.BuildTheNewCity.com

Build the New City!

How America Can Create Jobs and Meet the Challenges of the 21st Century

Build the New City!

How America Can Create Jobs and Meet the Challenges of the 21st Century

Todd Durant

Durant Publishing, LLC

Duncanville, Texas

Edited by Art Lizza.

Cover Design by Charlie Pabst of Charfish Design.

Copyedited by Ross Plotkin.

Durant Publishing, LLC
1238 Bow Creek Drive
Duncanville, Texas 75116

888 501-3033
Website: www.buildthenewcity.com

ISBN 978-0-578-11308-1 ebook
ISBN 978-0-578-11309-8 paperback

Printed in the United States of America

Acknowledgments

I want to especially thank my mother, who has always supported me in everything I have ever tried to accomplish. Thanks also to my son Trey and to Amy, my fiancée, who patiently listened to me talk incessantly about the New City over the past three years—and never asked me to shut up. And finally to Art, who gave me the confidence to think about the infinite possibilities of new ideas and made me believe that I wasn't just dreaming.

Contents

Introduction

This book issues a bold new challenge to America.

In many significant ways, our nation seems to be in a state of stagnation and polarization. Economically, for nearly four years we have been mired in a recession that shows few or no signs of improving in the immediate future. Nationwide unemployment hovers between eight and nine percent, with much higher rates in some states and major cities, while job growth remains poor or even nonexistent. Politically, perhaps at no point in our history have we seemed to be more sharply divided, even diametrically opposed, on virtually every issue that affects the American people, whether directly or indirectly. And America continues to be mired in wars and other military actions across the world—expensive campaigns in terms of lives and financial costs that sap our country's energy and resources, as well as impact our collective social conscience.

But as disturbing as all of this might sound, the thing that I find most troubling about America today has more to do with our country's spirit and soul—our national focus and our sense of purpose. I believe that for too long now, in the 11 years since 9/11, what might be defined as the national will has been strictly devoted to our "war on terror." Overseas, this focus has orchestrated wars in Iraq and Afghanistan, and military involvement in nearly a dozen other countries from Libya and Egypt to Pakistan and Yemen. Domestically, it has deflated our sense of promise and freedom through terror scares, burdensome security measures in cities and airports, and through endless debates over the degree to which personal liberties must be sacrificed in the name of homeland security and antiterrorism. One can make a strong argument that in many respects the defining focus of our nation is on war abroad and self-defense at home—even given the fact that in this election year most Americans report that their main concern is the lagging economy and the need for more and better jobs. It's a dismal picture, to be sure.

At the same time, America faces another new and ominous threat. It does not come from some superpower nation equipped with nuclear weapons aimed at us, and it does not come from a collection of fanatics—who might also have nuclear dirty bombs—hiding in caves in some desolate region or country, and who have vowed to destroy us. But this threat is quite real and potentially bigger, more powerful, and more devastating than any of that. And it comes from the Earth itself. It is called climate change, and the direct result of climate change is an ongoing, significant rise in ocean levels around the world that will cause severe flooding in many large coastal cities. Ultimately, unchecked rising sea levels will destroy part or all of many of those important cities.

Thus, a little more than a decade into the 21st century, America faces at least three formidable challenges: (1) Job creation and the "firing up" our economic machine to its former glory; (2) If I may paraphrase Abraham Lincoln, we must bind up the nation's social and political wounds, and deal forthrightly with those divisive issues and arguments that have torn us apart; and (3) The nation must accept the scientific validity of rising oceans and act immediately and proactively by developing plans for relocating large populations of people that are presently living in harm's way in low-lying, coastal flood zones.

Why not solve all three problems at the same time?

America needs a new peacetime challenge. We need a new national project. One that will unite the people of our country in mind and spirit, and one that will excite the imagination of just about everyone, young or old, who has ever wondered what marvelous things mankind can achieve when we set our minds and our wills to the task.

I am proposing that America set a goal of building a completely new, ultramodern city from the ground up—literally and figuratively—and fully populating that city within a span of ten years.

Think about how exciting and inspiring such a project would be: An entire, ultramodern city, completely preplanned, entirely wired for modern telecommunications systems, designed with people-moving capability from mass transit to bicycle routes to pedestrian access, and using green technology to minimize environmental impact and even eliminate pollution. In this book, I detail how all of this can be done, and also the range of benefits that such a project will provide, including:

✦ Job creation/economic development

✦ A range of affordable housing for different income levels

✦ Educational-system improvement

✦ Infrastructure improvement

◆A whole new export industry for U.S. companies (building New Cities in foreign countries)

◆Relocation of possibly millions of people from harm's way in low-lying coastal areas

◆Environmental reclamation of "clean" coastal/tidal areas

Yet the most valuable and longest-lasting benefit building the New City will generate is an enormous boost in the pride, morale, and outlook of the nation. The New City will create unprecedented national buzz and excitement based not on the fear and anxiety of the war on terror, but based on positive aspirations of accomplishing something— together—that will be a real benefit to people and a source of pride for Americans everywhere. It will be a massive peacetime investment into infrastructure development here at home rather than the continued spiral of military spending on weaponry and war material that is ultimately shipped overseas, much of it destroyed or later abandoned at the conclusion of the conflict.

What a fantastic macro-project building the New City will be for America!

An important goal—and an impetus for the writing of this book—is to get people involved and to seek out great ideas from people of all walks of life for building the New City and making their own individual contributions to getting America moving again economically, as well as helping to restore our national pride and spirit. As you read this book, I encourage you to go to the website www.BuildThe NewCity.com to post and share your ideas. Let's make this a national effort, and a project "By Americans For Americans."

Part I –
Why Do We Need to
Build the New City?

Chapter 1 - The New City Project and Job Creation

In this book I propose the creation of a new national focus and of a common worthwhile goal for the country—and specifically one that is NOT war, or war related. America's greatness is best illustrated by those times when all citizens were able to unite behind a single goal, to work together, hand in hand, toward an achievement that one way or another would be to the benefit of everyone in the nation—and to some extent, the entire world. I am talking about the causes that have served to unify the nation behind a single purpose with the resolve to succeed and not accept failure.

Now to be sure, in some of the instances of our greatest achievements the goals that I am referring to have in fact been war related, or have been in response to threats posed to our nation. Certainly our response to 9/11 was one such remarkable instance of Americans uniting as a nation to deal with the threat of worldwide terrorism and potential attacks at home and abroad. The same can assuredly be said for the way that America mobilized after the attack on Pearl Harbor to defeat the Axis in World War II. And of course there is much to be said for how Americans rolled up their sleeves and got to work in the factories and fields to win WWII, and to create a response that would prevent another 9/11 from ever happening, both of which I will discuss later in this book.

But I also think of peacetime crusades that have galvanized the country to rally around and embrace the effort to achieve a singular and sometimes spectacular goal. I think of 1961, when President Kennedy challenged America to land a man on the moon by the end of the decade, and we did. I think of the economic programs of FDR's New Deal, the Tennessee Valley Authority (TVA), and the Hoover Dam, which put Americans to work building infrastructure that would benefit all of us. I also think of situations in which the nation's conscience actually failed to mobilize its resolve and its resources to address what I believe should have been a national initiative—for example, in New Orleans after Hurricane Katrina.

Response to the Great Depression

The Great Depression and World War II are generally regarded as the most important economic events of the 20th century, and they are largely responsible for shaping the fiscal landscape of modern America to this day. And in a very striking way, these two major events seem to parallel our national situation today. Each of them—more particularly, America's response to depression and war in the 20th century—offers a lesson that might help us deal with our problems and challenges in the 21st century. These include the most serious recession since the Great Depression, and the serious threat some of our major cities and coastal areas face from continually rising seas.

In 1939, the United States was still deeply mired in the disastrous effects of the Great Depression. After 1929, the American Gross Domestic Product declined steadily for four straight years, and did not exceed the 1929 levels until 1936. The New Deal policies of Franklin Roosevelt mitigated some of the economic hardships the country was facing, although they did not end the economic crisis.

But it is interesting to look at some of the specific projects that were spawned during the Depression and the New Deal. The building of the Hoover Dam, for example, was started in April 1931 and completed in March 1936, two years ahead of schedule. According to the U.S. Department of the Interior's Bureau of Reclamation, a total of 21,000 men worked on the dam, with an average workforce of about 3,500 daily, which sometimes exceeded 5,000 workers at a time. Across the country, the TVA project was begun in 1933. At its peak in early 1942, according to the Authority's website, with 12 hydroelectric projects and a steam plant all under construction at the same time, the total TVA employment in design and construction topped 28,000 (http://www.tva.com/abouttva/history.htm).

I should point out that these figures represent direct employment at the Hoover Dam and by the TVA. There are no specific figures detailing how many manufacturing, supply, or factory jobs were created nationwide in support of those efforts, nor any proving how the local economies in numerous towns and counties flourished by supporting the workers and their families with food, clothing, and housing. This is important because a key component of the philosophy behind building the New City is to keep as many of the jobs that the project will create here in the United States.

It is also interesting to think of these government-sponsored projects as the "stimulus" programs of the 1930s, and perhaps even to admire how they seemingly did a better job of putting people to work than our modern stimulus programs, not to mention the big-bank and corporation bailouts—which also seem to have had few positive results creating good American jobs. Coincidently, the national unemployment rate in 2012 is essentially the same as it was during the Great Depression of the 1930s!

Mobilization for World War II

Ultimately, of course, World War II did effectively end the Depression. During the war years from 1941 to1945, the American economy expanded at an unprecedented rate as the gross national product (as measured in constant dollars) ballooned from $88.6 billion in 1939 to $135 billion in 1944, a prodigious rate of growth that has never been duplicated (Milward, 1979).

Unemployment

Perhaps the best measure of the dire economic consequences of the Great Depression—and the one that most parallels the situation in which we find ourselves today—are the unemployment rates at the time. According to the U.S. Bureau of Labor Statistics, as late as 1940, 11 years after the Crash of 1929, unemployment in the U.S. stood at 8.1% of the population and at a whopping 14.6% of the labor force.

Conversely, the effect of America's mobilization for the war was staggeringly swift and dramatic, particularly in the impact it had on reducing unemployment to virtually negligible levels. By 1943, the unemployment rate as a percentage of the population dropped to 1.1%, and by 1944 it was 0.7%; as a percentage of the labor force, the unemployment rate was 1.9% in 1943, and 1.2% the following year (see Table 1). That was a record low in American history; and even today, many economic experts agree that the 1.2% figure was as close to the concept of "full employment" that one could actually achieve.

Table 1: Civilian Employment and Unemployment During World War II (Numbers in thousands)

		1940	1941	1942	1943	1944	1945
All Non-Institutional Civilians		99,840	99,900	98,640	94,640	93,220	94,090
Civilian Labor Force	Total	55,640	55,910	56,410	55,540	54,630	53,860
	% of Population	55.7%	56%	57.2%	58.7%	58.6%	57.2%
Employed	Total	47,520	50,350	53,750	54,470	53,960	52,820
	% of Population	47.6%	50.4%	54.5%	57.6%	57.9%	56.1%
	% of Labor Force	85.4%	90.1%	95.3%	98.1%	98.8%	98.1%
Unemployed	Total	8,120	5,560	2,660	1,070	670	1,040
	% of Population	8.1%	5.6%	2.7%	1.1%	0.7%	1.1%
	% of Labor Force	14.6%	9.9%	4.7%	1.9%	1.2%	1.9%

Source: Bureau of Labor Statistics, "Employment status of the civilian noninstitutional population, 1940 to date." Available at http://www.bls.gov/cps/cpsaat1.pdf.

Building an Entire "New City"

One might be tempted to look at these job-creation numbers from the Great Depression and WWII and judge them paltry by contemporary standards. However, they were very significant figures back in the 1930s and 1940s. And both the Hoover Dam project and the TVA involved very specific industries for very specific tasks—the building of dams and plants for hydroelectric-power production as well as flood control and river management.

America today needs a tremendous number of jobs, and they must be good, well-paying ones that will improve the living standards of all Americans. So imagine with me if you will, the highly sophisticated and intensely coordinated process of constructing an ultramodern city in ten years— from scratch, from the ground up—in fact this very concept boggles the imagination. Everything from architecturally designing the micro and macro levels; constructing office and retail buildings right alongside residential spaces (both individual housing and apartments or condominiums); creating all infrastructure, power plants, and telecommunications; providing schools and universities; developing transportation hubs from new airports to rail stations; erecting hospitals and government-service complexes; and so forth.

All of this will require a massive workforce. For example, consider the worker requirements for individual construction projects today. The new Denver International Airport alone, completed in 1995, employed over 11,000 workers. The Port Authority of New York and New Jersey estimates that there are currently 3,500 workers rebuilding the World Trade Center site in lower Manhattan. According to the Nuclear Energy Institute (NEI), building a new nuclear-energy plant will create up to 3,500 jobs—and once completed, that facility will provide 400 to 700 long-term positions at salaries that are typically 36% higher than the local average. (The NEI website also underscores the U.S. Department of Energy's projection that the United States will require 22% more electricity by the year 2035.)

Now imagine all of this effort going on at once. We are talking about hundreds of thousands of quality jobs being created across the country. Of course, the vast majority of those jobs will likely be in and around the site chosen for the location of the New City. However, from technical expertise right down to the manufacture of prefabricated materials needed to build the physical city, thousands of other jobs will be created in support of the New City project.

South Korea's Songdo International Business District (IBD)

Sound crazy? Are you still a skeptic? Then consider South Korea's Songdo IBD project in Incheon Province, 20 miles west of Seoul, which is *already under construction.* The first phase of the city opened on August 7, 2009. Located on 1,500 acres of reclaimed land on the Incheon waterfront, Songdo is the $35 billion visionary "smart" city, or "technopolis," of developer Stanley C. Gale, and the largest private real-estate development in history. The project is massive: When it is completed in 2017, it will have 80,000 apartments (it is intriguing that some Japanese survivors of the 2011 Tōhoku earthquake have already sought apartments in Songdo); forty million square feet of office space; thirty-five million square feet of residential space; ten million square feet of retail space; five million square feet of hotel space; and ten million square feet of public space. The IBD city is planned for a daytime population of 300,000, and a permanent-resident population of 65,000 (Engineering News Record, 2011).

A virtual nervous system of computer technology and telecommunications will link everyone who lives and works in Songdo, and in a way, the residences and buildings themselves. That's because all of the construction will be infused with networked "artificial intelligence"— sometimes called "ambient intelligence"—managed by a master grid. In this way, Songdo will truly be a "smart city" in every sense. In computing, *ambient intelligence* is a term used to describe an electronically equipped environment that is sensitive to the presence of people and responsive to their tasks and activities. Think of HAL 9000 in the movie *2001: A Space Odyssey*—ambient-intelligence devices will be fully integrated into the environment and work in concert with people engaged in carrying out their daily functions, activities, and rituals.

Additionally, the city is the spearhead of South Korea's commitment to promote green-buildings construction and low carbon growth, right down to a system of trash removal that eliminates the need for garbage hauling via truck. If completed as planned, Songdo IBD will be the first major city in the world in which all of the major buildings either meet or exceed all Leadership in Energy and Environment Design (LEED) requirements.

I will discuss the technological, ambient-intelligence innovations and the green, LEEDs aspects that will be incorporated into the building of the New City in a later chapter. For now I would like remain focused in this chapter on the issue of job creation, and especially to highlight some of the most pertinent facts relating to the Songdo IBD project. By the close of 2011, over 100 LEED certified buildings had been completed, with 229 additional buildings still under construction and over 50,000 workers onsite, according to Mary Lou DiNardo, a spokesperson for Gale International.

Now I ask: Isn't this something that we could be doing right here in the U.S.? Gale International, the developer of Songdo IBD, is an American company that, in partnership with Morgan Stanley, holds a 70% stake in the estimated $40 billion project (the remaining 30% stake is owned by POSCO, a South Korean steel company). Furthermore, I want to emphasize the fact that Songdo is a privately funded development project; no government or taxpayer dollars are being used for its construction and development. I believe that should be a model for the New City in America, and I will have more to say about that later in this book as well.

Still don't believe? Here is another example happening in a foreign country.

Tatu City, Kenya

Another very interesting and ambitious smart city is the Tatu City project on the African continent, which is currently being built from scratch in Kenya on 2,400 acres of old coffee-plantation land less than 25 minutes from both the city proper of Nairobi and Jomo Kenyatta International Airport, and only a few miles from Kenyatta University. The project is similar in scope to Songdo in that it is expected to provide homes for 70,000 new residents in middle- to high-income housing units (there is some vagueness about the provision of low-income housing) with about 30,000 workforce and tourist visitors on a daily basis. All told, according to estimates, Tatu City will provide over 220,000 short-term construction jobs and over 115,000 permanent ones (www.TatuCity.com).

But even beyond the fundamental benefit of massive job creation, Tatu is an intriguing smart-city project for a variety of other reasons as well.

The first and foremost is that under the auspices of the Nairobi Metro 2030 Strategy, which is part of a wider national development initiative for the country, the masterminds behind Tatu City are promoting it as a project undertaken in Kenya—by Kenyans for Kenyans. And, in fact, much of the capital funding and support is coming from sources within Kenya. This approach goes right to the heart of my vision for the building of the New City in America. How fantastic would it be to have a grand project that is designed specifically for the benefit of all Americans —by Americans for Americans—which will in turn benefit the entire country economically and socially?

The second reason that the Tatu City project is worth looking at is that, like Songdo, it is also being built through private investment, not with government or taxpayer money (except for some funded infrastructure improvements that will connect the city to new highways and other facilities). As I mentioned with respect to Songdo, it will be important to limit or restrict government involvement in the construction and development of the New City both to keep partisan politics out of the picture and to prevent taxpayers from footing the bill to build it.

However, there is another interesting wrinkle in the private-funding mix of Tatu City: the principal backer of the project is the Moscow-based Renaissance Partners, one of the world's largest emerging-markets investment banks. Given the history of our country's fierce competition with the former Soviet Union over the course of the decades-long Cold War, as well as in the Space Race and many other areas of endeavor, wouldn't many older Americans just love an opportunity to beat the Russians in the quest to build the first ultramodern, ultra-smart New City? I believe the answer is obvious.

Another noteworthy aspect of Tatu City is that, while it is envisioned as a completely preplanned "new city" and is being built "from scratch," it is also hoped that it will help ease overcrowding in greater Nairobi (Kenya's capital, and with about three million people, the most populous city in East Africa). That is, the gleaming new Tatu City is expected to attract people to relocate from the more crowded districts of Nairobi with the result of redistributing the residents more evenly throughout Nairobi County.

Now, at over a mile above sea level and about 300 miles from the ocean, Nairobi is certainly in no danger of being flooded by rising seas, but the expectations for Tatu City point to another benefit of building the New City in America (perhaps more than one). Many of America's older coastal cities also suffer from overcrowding coupled with limited housing—even to the point of critical housing shortages. And while one of the main goals of the New City is to move people out of harm's way in the low-lying danger zones that will inevitably be inundated by rising sea levels, another probable result is that some residents of relatively safe areas of coastal cities—those on higher ground, for instance—will also relocate to the New City in search of better living conditions, better schools, and better-paying jobs. Thus, in this way, the New City will help to redistribute the residential population in America, easing overcrowding in some of our major older cities and increasing the quality of life for many Americans.

Another aspect of Tatu City that I want to point out is that, again like Songdo, the city will feature extensive quality-of-life amenities. For example, 35% of the land will be set aside as natural greenbelt areas and maintained as wetland, and 15% will be devoted to world-class schools, hospitals, and infrastructure—the same formula that appears to be working so successfully in Songdo (provided the developers follow Songdo's lead and build the people-friendly components first).

New City: The Biggest and the Best

To give you an idea of the magnitude of scale that I am talking about, you need to consider that according to varying estimates, both Songdo and Tatu City are being built to accommodate somewhere between 60,000 and 80,000 residents. That is not nearly enough for the New City; and more importantly, I believe it is not nearly enough for *America's* New City. Instead, I envision building a city to house at least a half million residents and to accommodate an additional half million visitors, including both tourists and businesspeople. Extrapolating from the numbers of positions that have actually been created by Songdo and Tatu City, Table 2 displays the tremendous potential for job creation by the New City.

These numbers are of course just estimates, and it is difficult to precisely ascertain the kind of job-generation potential that the New City will actually have. However, as we have seen in such instances as the war effort, once you jump-start the American economic machine, ambitious, enterprising people and corporations seem to find more and more ways to get down to work. Energy and enthusiasm drive entrepreneurship and innovation. Look again at the way the war effort drove unemployment from eight percent to below one percent. Inasmuch as I truly like the idea of throwing down a massive challenge to America, given the potential of job creation from building the New City, what do you think about constructing *two* of them?

TABLE 2. POTENTIAL JOB CREATION IN BUILDING
THE NEW CITY

PROJECT TYPE	ESTIMATED NUMBER OF JOBS
City Construction	100,000–150,000
Airport	10,000–12,000
Rail Station	8,000–10,000
Nuclear-Power Plant	3,500–4,500
Water-Delivery Plant	3,000–4,000
Wastewater-Treatment Facility	3,000–4,000
Trucking/Delivery of Materials	1,000–1,500
NATIONWIDE	
Manufacturing (Building materials)	40,000–50,000
Technical/Engineering/ Architectural	5,000–10,000
Environmental-Habitat Restoration	20,000–30,000
Total Estimated Job Creation	**193,500–276,000**

A Call to Action

I want to conclude this chapter by asking a question: What is the most important lesson to be learned from these examples? The apparent success of the Songdo and Tatu City projects, at least in their early stages, raises an issue that is at the heart of the challenge I present in this book. Other countries, and large corporations and banks therein, are embarking upon the successful development and construction of the most magnificent and technologically advanced super-cities ever built. Is America going to stand by and simply watch as the first fully integrated smart cities are successfully built in foreign countries—at least one of which is being underwritten by a Russian company? Where is our sense of pride of accomplishment? Where is our competitive spirit, striving to be the first to produce the next great innovation, the next great leap in human achievement? I am talking about the kinds of achievements that change the way we see and think and move about in the world, such as the first manned lunar landing in 1969, when millions of Americans sat mesmerized in front of their television sets holding their collective breath; or the Manhattan Project, which both ended WWII and forever changed the way that we generate electricity to power our cities and towns, businesses and homes. Are we going to let other nations beat us in the race to create the next generation of great "smart cities"? Or are we going to get into the game and win?

Writing in *Better! Cities and Towns*, former U.S. Secretary of Housing and Urban Development Henry Cisneros has said of the U.S.:

It is clear that demand for infrastructure of all kinds will grow. The Census Bureau estimates the population will grow by 30%, from 306 million in 2009 to 395 million, by 2050. Moreover, we are on the front edge of an "urban age" in human history—a period of metropolitan emergence and city renaissance worldwide. In the U.S., according to the Brookings Institution, 65% of the nation's population lives in the top 100 metro areas, which in turn produce 75% of national GDP, 76% of knowledge jobs, 78% of patent activity, and 78% of research dollars.

Can there ever be a better time to build the New City than right now? Is there any better country to build it than America?

Go to the website www.BuildTheNewCity.com and post your ideas!

Chapter 2 - The Facts About Rising Seas

For at least the last decade or so, there has been an ongoing and often heated debate over whether the Earth's average temperature is slowly increasing in a process often referred to as "global warming." The flashpoint of the debate (and the issue that has seemed to elicit the most angry and passionate arguments, responses, claims, and rebuttals) regarded whether global warming is the result of natural forces at work within and on the surface of the planet—or whether mankind, at least in part, is responsible for contributing to global warming through a number of activities, from the creation of greenhouse gases to the destruction of vast habitats (such as rainforests) that would serve to mitigate those gases through both the consumption of carbon dioxide and the production of oxygen.

The debate may have reached its crescendo with the release by former Vice President Al Gore of the documentary *An Inconvenient Truth* in 2006, by which time the whole issue had become highly politicized, with candidates and office seekers (most of whom were not the least bit scientifically qualified to offer an opinion) weighing in on one side or the other, most of whom were not the least bit scientifically qualified to so much as offer an opinion. Today the tone of the debate has changed somewhat, with the term "global warming" largely replaced with the perhaps less inflammatory phrase "climate change." The fact remains, as we will see in this chapter, that the phenomenon of rising seas is real, and millions of people in the United States are increasingly at risk of disaster from worsening flooding during hurricanes or other severe coastal-storm events.

I do not wish to get embroiled in the debate over whether the documented climate changes that are happening to the Earth are the result of natural forces or are caused directly or indirectly by man's activities, or a combination of those factors. Nor will I engage in any speculation as to whether this planet's average temperature will continue to rise or not. That remains to be seen.

However, one of the main points that I focus on in this book, and which I see as one of the many very powerful and compelling reasons for building the New City— perhaps the single strongest one from a humanitarian perspective—is that it has been factually proven that world sea levels are rising, consequently threatening important, low-lying coastal cities everywhere. My biggest concern, of course, is the threat posed by rising seas to coastal towns and major cities throughout the U.S. The rising of ocean levels around the world is a documented scientific fact, and it is a phenomenon that is quantifiable and thus empirically measurable. The word "empirically" means "observable"— in other words, we can actually see that the seas are rising and measure both how much they are rising and how fast.

I leave it to others to debate the causes. What I see, and what most earth scientists see, is an impending crisis, or a series of crises in cities all around the country, some of which will face complete destruction with just a three-foot rise in sea levels. A sobering fact is that some projections predict much higher jumps than that. But I also see a fantastic solution in the creation and the building of the New City through which we can meet the challenge head on. We must respond proactively to this ominous threat to our shores by providing a haven to relocate the perhaps hundreds of thousands of people who will inevitably be displaced by the destructive impact of rising seas.

In this chapter, I present scientific data to prove that rising sea levels are a fact—and that we ought to be concerned.

The Scientific Case

For a long time, earth scientists looked to the skies to try to understand climate change around the world. That is, they studied atmospheric phenomena in an effort to explain the fluctuations in average temperatures around the globe, as well as the receding of ice shelves and glaciers at both the Arctic and Antarctic poles. What they found was a significant increase in atmospheric carbon-dioxide levels. A recent study by Jeremy Shakun et al. (2012), published in *Nature*, found that carbon-dioxide levels have risen by about 100 parts-per-million (ppm) since the end of the last ice age about 10,000 years ago. In a BBC News article (bbc.co.uk/news/science-environment-17611404), lead author Shakun said, "At the end of the last ice age, carbon dioxide rose from about 180 parts per million (ppm) in the atmosphere to about 260; and today we're at 392. So, in the last 100 years we've gone up about 100 ppm—about the same as at the end of the last ice age. . . . Rising carbon dioxide at the end of the ice age had a huge effect on global climate."

However, in more recent years, scientists have begun to understand the significant role that warming ocean temperatures are playing in driving Antarctic ice loss and the shrinking of Arctic glaciers, particularly in Greenland. Using a laser altimeter onboard NASA's ICESat satellite, scientists discovered thinning and shrinkage of Antarctic ice shelves—the floating plates of ice that jut out from the land—that could not be explained simply by warmer air temperatures. What they discovered was that warmer currents undermine glacial ice shelves from underneath, resulting in more calving of icebergs into the sea, sometimes in spectacular fashion. A case in point is occurring in Greenland, where a 46-square-mile chunk (the size of Manhattan) broke away from the Petermann Glacier in July 2012—although this was dwarfed by an ice chunk *four times its size* that had dislodged from the same glacier two years earlier. In Antarctica, researchers from the Alfred Wegener Institute for Polar and Marine Research in Germany are concerned that the nearly 174,000-square-mile Filchner-Ronne Ice Shelf that rims the Weddell Sea is under threat. Their calculations indicate that the giant ice shelf will disintegrate by the end of the century.

Naturally, as these giant icebergs float away and melt, they add volumes of water to the oceans. But there is much more to the situation than that, because polar ice shelves act as buffers that protect the much larger glaciers that sit on land from being eroded by these warmer ocean waters. As Dr. Hartmut Hellmer of the Wegener Institute describes it,

"Ice shelves are like corks in the bottles for the ice streams behind them. They reduce the ice flow. If, however, the ice shelves melt from below, they become so thin that the dragging surfaces become smaller and the ice behind them starts to move" (www.reuters.com/article/2012/05/09/us-antarctica-global-warming-idUSBRE84811E20120509). This is happening to at least 20 major ice shelves in Antarctica that are being melted from below by warm ocean currents, some of which show thinning of up to 23 feet per year.

And as those "corks" melt, the giant glaciers behind them start to move faster into the ocean because the shelves simply no longer have the massive force to hold back the glacial floes. Satellite surveys from the years 2000 to 2011 of more than 200 glaciers in Greenland indicate that many of the ice floes to the east, southeast, and northwest have increased their speed by an average of 30%; some of them are traveling as much as seven miles per year (Zabarenko, 2012). All of this action combined is dumping billions of gallons of water into the world's oceans. Current scientific estimates show that global sea levels rose over .5 inches between the years 2003 and 2010, primarily due to melting ice shelves and glaciers. A further rise of nearly .7 inches is attributed to the expansion of the oceans as the water warms.

We are already seeing the impact of these elevated sea levels. In the South Pacific, the low-lying island nation of Kiribati, which consists of a series of islands near Australia on which 100,000 people live, is slowly disappearing under the sea. An entire nation will, in effect, be swallowed up by the ocean. Across the world in the Indian Ocean, the islands of the Maldives and the Seychelles face a similar watery fate, and these examples profoundly illustrate that rising sea levels are a worldwide phenomenon that cannot be ignored. In the U.S., large portions of the Everglades are disappearing, and the flooding that occurs in coastal areas during natural disasters such as Hurricane Katrina has been getting more severe and pervasive every year.

Hellmer and his team predict that the melting of just the Filchner-Ronne Ice Shelf could add up to 1.7 inches per year to rising global sea levels. The scientists who conducted the satellite survey of the Greenland glaciers postulate that a rise of eight inches in ocean levels around the world is very possible. And even a slight rise in the levels of the oceans along low-lying coastal areas can be devastating by making it easier for hurricanes and other weather disasters to push more seawater ashore and farther inland. In Louisiana, the situation is further compounded by the fact that just as the seas are rising, the land along the coast is sinking. It isn't any wonder that the Louisiana Gulf region is the one most at risk of being wiped out or made uninhabitable by rising seas. At the same time, of course, New Orleans and the surrounding area will perhaps be one of the prime regions in the country—though certainly not the only one—to benefit from America's building of the New City.

And if an increase in the world's overall ocean level of an inch or two doesn't strike you as alarming, consider the fact that sea levels are rising faster and higher along 600 miles of the eastern seaboard of the United States from Cape

Hatteras, North Carolina to just north of Boston—some of the most expensive and urbanized coastal real estate in the world. The U.S. Geological Survey, which has been studying and recording ocean level change around American shores since 1950, reports that sea levels along this entire region are rising at an annual rate that is three to four times faster than the global average (Sallenger, Jr., Doran, & Howd, 2012).

This disturbing trend began to take hold in 1990, and according to the study's lead author, oceanographer Asbury H. Sallenger, Jr., not only is the sea along this stretch rising faster than the rest of the world, the process is happening at a faster pace. So consider the numbers: While the average global rise in sea levels since 1990 stands at about 2.0 inches, the USGS research over that same period shows a sea-level rise in Norfolk, Virginia of 4.8 inches; in Philadelphia of 3.7 inches; and in New York City of 2.8 inches.

The reason these East Coast figures are staggeringly higher than the worldwide average is that global warming alters the pattern of ocean currents, most importantly by slowing them down. As that happens, the slope of the seas changes to compensate for the slowing current, which in turn pushes up sea levels along the northeast coast of the U.S. Previous computer models had predicted such a probability, but this latest USGS survey data was the first research to confirm that this is already happening.

In its 2007 report, the Intergovernmental Panel on Climate Change (IPCC) projected a rise in ocean levels of between 7.1 and 23 inches by the year 2100. More recently, a National Research Council report released in June 2012 projects that by the year 2100 the California coast will experience an average three-foot rise in sea level while Oregon and Washington State will see an average two-foot rise. Imagine the devastation that such a catastrophe would ultimately cause from San Diego and Los Angeles up to San Francisco and Seattle, as well as to countless coastal towns in between!

Earlier in this chapter, I said that from a humanitarian perspective, the fact that sea levels are rising around the world is probably the most important reason to build the New City. I firmly believe that each of the reasons that I present in this book—job creation; powering a new, prosperous economy; creating a unifying national goal that will benefit the country as a whole; and so on—stand on their own to justify the New City. Plainly stated, every single one of the major reasons that I present in this book is, in my opinion, sufficiently compelling enough on its own merits to justify the building of the New City.

However, it is certainly also quite clearly the case that the threat of rising sea levels inevitably swamping coastal cities and towns poses the greatest risk to human life, and has the greatest potential for catastrophe. And if you think that this threat is way off in the future, and thus not something we need to worry about now, you need to reconsider. While it is true that the seas are rising gradually, and many studies predict that the inundations of two to three feet in the hardest-hit coastal areas will build slowly until about the year 2100, the major threat today is from the increased severity of flood damage from hurricanes and other weather-related disasters.

In a recent *New York Times* article ("Rising Sea Levels Seen as Threat to Coastal U.S.," March 13, 2012), Justin Gillis reported on demographic surveys, based on the latest U.S. Census figures, which indicate that 3.7 million Americans live within a few feet of high tide—the very areas that will be hit most severely with coastal flooding made worse by even a single inch of ocean-level rise (Strauss, Ziemlinski, Weiss, & Overpeck, 2012; Tebaldi, Strauss, & Zervas, 2012). In other words, even slight rises in the sea level result in exponentially greater damage to property and, yes, loss of life as well. Every incremental increase in the ocean level creates greater and fiercer storm surges, which in turn push the flooding farther inland, doing billions more in damage, and increasing the magnitude of human suffering. Gillis quotes one of the authors of the two studies, Benjamin H. Strauss, who said, "Sea-level rise is like an invisible tsunami, building force while we do almost nothing. We have a closing window of time to prevent the worst by preparing for higher seas." These scientists predict that what we once categorized as 100-year or 50-year storms could quickly become every-few-years occurrences in the next few decades (See Figure 1).

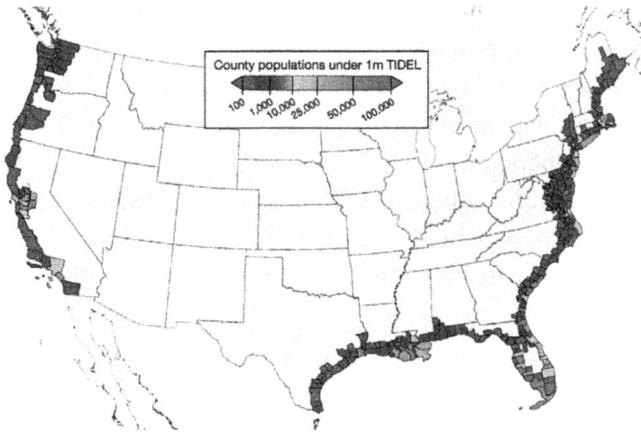

Figure 1. Populations living on land less than 1 meter above local mean high water mark (From Strauss, et al., 2012. Reprinted with permission.)

Strauss and his colleagues hope that their research findings, which indicate that millions of Americans are increasingly at risk from such disasters, will both help to make the public more aware of these dangerous realities and inspire the country to take action to prevent such unpredictable catastrophes. I heartily agree, and part of my purpose in this book is to foster a nationwide discussion of these issues, as well as to offer some solutions. The rising level of the oceans, however incremental, is seriously affecting us *right now*. It has already cost governments and private landowners billions of dollars in property damage, and what are simply futile attempts to preserve or restore eroding beaches by perpetually pumping megatons of sand onto them, only to have them washed out again during the next storm season. In the *New York Times* article, Gillis writes, "For decades, coastal scientists have argued that these policies are foolhardy, and that the nation must begin planning an orderly retreat from large portions of its coasts, but few politicians have been willing to embrace that message or to warn the public of the rising risks."

Again, I heartily agree. Moreover, I believe that the New City offers at least a part of the solution by providing an extremely plausible relocation option for residents of the danger areas along our coastlines, who I reiterate are *3.7 million people*! Strauss and his colleagues predict that all U.S. coastal areas below the 3.3 ocean-level line will eventually be permanently inundated—so the time to act is now. Life for people in those regions will become a series of one disaster after another, and rebuilding will be both monumentally expensive and futile. It would also be irresponsible to leave residents there, knowing as we do that all of those rebuilding efforts are very likely to be washed away by the next severe storm.

Just think of the colossal waste of money this represents, as well as the extent of the disruption to human lives it causes. It has now been over seven years since Hurricane Katrina—the costliest hurricane disaster ever in the U.S. at $81 billion—and to this day we are still not finished with the rebuilding effort in New Orleans. Do we really wish to continue doing this, or is there a viable alternative?

Instead, I propose that we build the New City. What are your ideas? Throughout this book, I ask for readers' input. I do not pretend to have all of the answers; but I want, as I said earlier, to encourage and promote some sort of dialogue or discussion or debate through which Americans can put their heads together and come up with great ideas and potential solutions to meet these serious challenges head-on. I invite you to go to the website www.BuildTheNewCity.com and post your thoughts and ideas. Let's get people talking about these issues, because if we do, I am certain we will be able to develop some really innovative strategies and plans to proactively meet the challenges America faces.

Chapter 3 – Creating a National Buzz

Earlier in Chapter 1 of this book, I talked about the spectacular way that our country responded to the threat of World War II—how we mobilized our resources and became unified and totally committed to winning the war and preserving our freedom and our very way of life. Economically the effects of that commitment are most easily seen in the record 54% jump in the GNP in the space of five years, and the achievement of near-zero unemployment for perhaps the only time in U.S. history.

Most of us are to some degree aware, from our history books and classes in school, of the tremendous military buildup that was required to meet the challenge of winning the war. To mention only one example, the United States shipbuilding industry, which had actually been in a severe depression since 1921 (long before the Crash of 1929), had produced only 71 ships from 1930 to 1936, the year that Franklin Roosevelt authorized the U.S. Maritime Commission (USMC) to revive the shipbuilding industry. Under the USMC, America then turned out 106 ships between 1938 and 1940, and almost that same number in the single year of 1941 (Fischer, 1949).

We are also aware of some of the most remarkable feats of accomplishment that were successfully undertaken in the context of the war effort, such as the Manhattan Project and the technological innovations that came about in the aerospace industry (which would later fuel America's Mercury and Apollo exploratory programs). Yet few of us are probably aware of the vast array of very small (or more precisely—since really, no aspect of the war effort was "small" in terms of importance—the more *subtle*), behind-the-scenes things that were done by ordinary people, all pulling together to defeat the Axis. The U.S. automobile industry converted from manufacturing over three million cars in 1941 to turning out war equipment and machines (only 139 cars were built over the remaining duration of the war). And while the average automobile had about 15,000 parts, carmakers began rapidly producing airplanes such as the B-19 Liberator that had over one million parts—and doing it at the rate of one plane a minute! (See: http://www.pbs.org/thewar/at_home_war_production.htm) For another example, numerous movies have been made about wartime linguists, including Native American Navajos working night and day to crack enemy codes. American women went to work in droves in the manufacturing sector, filling the void left by men serving in the war. The list goes on and on.

World War II ended 67 years ago; and sadly, of course, there are fewer and fewer people alive today who remember what it must have been like to witness the country pulling together with a common cause and purpose, and becoming so unified in the process. More fresh in our minds today is the way America became unified, at least in spirit, after the 9/11 attacks in 2001. If we carefully examine the aftermath of 9/11, you will see that while it certainly had a unifying effect on all Americans, there was —and still is—a level of frustration with our response to that tragedy. The unity that most Americans felt in the days and years immediately thereafter has faded much more quickly than we all would have liked.

My reason for saying this is that it seems our frustration sprang from not really knowing *how* to respond to 9/11— what constructive action that we as individuals could take. We flew American flags from our homes and offices; we threw our support behind the President and the wars that were shortly thereafter waged in Iraq and Afghanistan; and we resigned ourselves to the inconvenience of tighter security measures here at home. As with the attack on Pearl Harbor, of course, many people of marching age joined the military or the reserves. But unlike WWII, there was really very little of substance that the average person could do beyond going on with his or her daily life.

Let us also face the reality that in so many ways, we Americans are ambivalent and even a little dissatisfied with our response to 9/11, further fueling our national frustration. We applaud the killing of Osama bin Laden and his henchmen, but we argue over the continued war in Afghanistan, and we still debate whether we should have invaded Iraq. There is tension from airport-screening rooms right up to the nation's courts as to how much invasive scrutiny private citizens must endure in the name of homeland security versus protecting the rights of liberty and freedom guaranteed by our Constitution.

And today we are back to our old divisive politics, still mired in an unpopular war in Afghanistan, and stuck in a seemingly perpetual recession that chokes our productivity; stifles job growth and prosperity; and severely dampens our national spirit and our pride in America. It is not a happy time in America.

An Incredible Peacetime National Goal

What I am proposing with my concept of the New City is perhaps one of the greatest and most collaborative peacetime projects in history. And by "collaborative," I mean a project whose factors include: The involvement of millions of Americans across a broad spectrum (in elements such as a proactive response and addressing the impending crisis of rising seas); good jobs both building the New City and supplying the technology and raw materials needed for it; and the best resources to populate and enervate the metropolis, making it into a world-class, technologically advanced "technopolis" in a shorter amount of time than has been accomplished ever before. This collaboration will involve both the public and private sectors of government and independent businesses; it will involve government on the federal, state, and local levels; it will involve business and industry from banking and investment to manufacturing and construction; and in a very practical and tangible way it will involve individual citizens in a myriad of ways that I detail throughout this book. Just consider the following overview.

Choosing the Site for the New City

I envision a process through which each of the 50 states is invited to submit bids for building the New City within its borders, much like the way the International Olympic Committee entertains bids from cities around the world to host the Winter and Summer Games every four years. The basic criteria in this process would most likely have to be very scientific in nature, drawing on hard factual data about environment and practicality—a kind of broad-based ergonomic assessment designed to pinpoint the potential sites around the country in which the New City would have the optimal chances to succeed economically and socially. The ideal is for the New City to emerge as an engine that drives the economy and the culture of the entire nation forward in ways that no single city in the United States—or the world, for that matter—ever has before.

Thus, for example, factors like adequate water resources to meet the needs of a million city residents, or the feasibility of connecting the New City's airport and rail-transportation hubs into the national grid are going to be key critical concerns that must be evaluated in the bidding process. Going a bit further, part of the New City plan will include the construction of a nuclear-power plant to supply the electricity needed by the city into the 22nd century. Consequently, the site that is chosen will need to be one that is also a safe place for a nuclear facility—sites that are near geographic fault lines will most likely have to be eliminated.

Clearly, the process of choosing the final, winning site on which to build the New City will be an extremely complicated and exhaustive process in which countless details will have to be evaluated and weighed in relative importance before the final determination can be made. But think about all of the advantages of starting completely from scratch and building a new, ultramodern, electronically interconnected, and completely preplanned city—the first step of which would be selecting the very best ground and location on which to put it. A uniformly new construction like this has rarely been attempted, and it boggles the mind just to think about it.

How would you vote if given the opportunity to choose the site for building 5he New City? Go to the website www.BuildTheNewCity.com and post your thoughts.

How Will We Select the People to Live in the New City?

This will be fun.

Let me begin on a more serious note. In Chapter 2, I discussed and documented the scientific facts that prove ocean levels around the world are steadily rising. The inevitable conclusion that you must draw from this scientific reality is that important, low-lying coastal areas of our country—including some heavily populated cities and towns—will be underwater and uninhabitable one day in the not-too-distant future. My plan is for the New City to be the primary relocation destination for anyone displaced by rising seas who wishes to reside in the most sophisticated metropolis every designed and built. That strikes me as a very exciting and very desirable proposition. Not only that, but in many cases, for people living in older U.S. cities beset by poverty, overcrowding, and a lack of jobs, good schools, and solid public transportation, the New City will provide an escape from all of these factors. Why wouldn't you want to move to the New City?

Having said that, it should be clear that it will not be practical or feasible to draw all of the new residents of the New City from these flooded coastal areas—nor would that be the most beneficial thing to do. The New City will require people from all walks of life, from every educational level, and with every manner of creative talent and expertise. It will require tradespeople and manufacturing workers; technicians and programmers; planners and developers; teachers and college professors; nurses and doctors; business professionals; and so on. With that in mind, I propose that we open the possibility of residing in the New City to every American citizen who might be even vaguely interested in doing so.

In fact, I want to take the attractive prospects of living and working in the New City even higher. I propose that we hold a national lottery to give away—free of charge—between five and ten percent of the residential spaces that are built. The spectrum of available homes could include modest apartments, condominiums, and private residences scattered throughout the New City. We will model this national lottery on what was done in this country with the Homestead Act of 1862. Under the Homestead Act, nearly any man or woman over 21 years old (or the head of a household) was given a parcel of roughly 160 acres of land (defined as a homestead) for a nominal fee. Some historians regard the Homestead Act as the most important law ever passed in the United States for the welfare of the people. You now have a better idea how vitally important the New City residence lottery will be to all who participate, and especially of course to those who are fortunate enough to win a new home.

The Homestead Act was not without political ramifications. The original legislation was blocked in

Congress by Southern Democrats who both wanted the Western lands for slave owners, and feared the eventual addition of antislavery states populated by "Free Soil" proponents supported by the Northern states. I mention this aspect to make a point: The lottery of residential spaces in the New City will be conducted free of any political constraints whatsoever. In fact, I envision several such lotteries conducted over the entire timeframe of the construction phase of the project.

Think about all of the media fanfare and crazy excitement that takes place across the country whenever one of the prizes in the really big lotteries like Mega Millions or Powerball reaches into the $200 or $300 million range—or higher! People form blocks-long lines queuing up to buy tickets; the media are all over it with local and national reporters everywhere covering the story; and millions of eternally optimistic hopefuls watch the drawing on television. And as soon as there is a winner (or winners), everybody in the country wants to know where the ticket was bought and the name of the recipient. Now imagine the kind of excitement and enthusiasm that will be created by a series of lotteries conducted over the 10 years of construction of the New City, with the prize being a brand-new, ultramodern apartment or house in the most technologically sophisticated city in the world! It will be enough to turn a one-minute lottery drawing into a TV reality show! And in fact, a reality show could also be a really exciting component of promoting and populating the New City!

To contribute your own ideas about how to invite or select the residents of the New City, go to the website www.BuildTheNewCity.com.

An American Challenge

In Chapter 1 I talked about Songdo in South Korea and Tatu City in Kenya and I asked the question *Is America going to stand by and simply watch as the first fully integrated smart cities are successfully built in foreign countries by foreign companies?* I believe that as Americans, we always want to be first. After being beaten by the Soviet Union when they achieved the first manned space flight, we rolled up our sleeves and got to work, and we became the first (and only) country to put a man on the moon. But this is not simply a matter of nationalistic egotism. It is important to remember that a great deal of new technological and practical innovations come out of these kinds of cutting-edge projects. I am referring to the kinds of simple innovations that make life easier for everyday people. Thousands of these spinoffs came out of the space program; we are not even aware of most of them, nor of even the simple ways that they impact our daily lives —call it the "Teflon and Tang effect," if you will, from two applicable inventions. It is important for America to lead the way in building the best, most technologically advanced New City because we must take advantage of everything that will be learned in the process, and all of the innovations and inventions that will be developed as a result, for they will benefit all Americans.

Furthermore, there is another crucial reason why America should lead the way in building the New City, one that will benefit virtually all Americans in most if not all of the 50 states. I envision that the New City will be completely American-made—all of the technology, all of the construction, all of the raw materials from concrete and steel to computer instrumentation and software will be supplied and built by U.S. companies. Every tree and shrub in the New City's parks and along its avenues will have been grown in American soil.

We will invite all interested American companies in all of the states to compete for the opportunity to be suppliers of the things that will go into the building of the city. First and foremost, this will ensure that the prosperity and jobs afforded by the building of the New City will be spread to states, companies, and workers across the country. As a matter of pride, we would endeavor to acknowledge, in some small way, the various contributions of companies and organizations to the project. So for example, the companies that fabricated the steel might be honored with plaques inscribed with their names, to be placed in the lobbies or on the cornerstones of those buildings. In a broad sense—in a nationwide sense—the New City will be very much a project "by Americans for Americans."

I also firmly believe that America must take the lead in building the first technopolis (and the ones to follow) because we will do it better than anyone else. For example, despite its apparent success so far, Songdo has been criticized because it is being built along the Incheon waterfront on land that was reclaimed from the Yellow Sea!

This despite the scientifically documented and proven fact that sea levels around the world are continually rising, as I discussed in Chapter 2. That is certainly an obvious and major mistake that will certainly not be made with the American New City site. But more than that, I believe that American companies are better equipped, and American urban planners better informed, than any comparable professionals in the world—and thus the most able to anticipate problems and avoid critical errors in the conception and development of the New City.

Nor does American involvement end there. Because once the first New City is successfully constructed in America, it is likely that there will be a strong demand to build others —if not in America, certainly in other places around the world where many coastal cities are in even greater danger of utter destruction from rising sea levels and where the problem of urban overcrowding cities is at or approaching crisis stage. The companies and developers that take a leadership role in building the American New City will have a massive opportunity to export a brand-new product —a complete turnkey technopolis, from scratch, from the ground up—constructing ultramodern cities that will elevate the quality of life for millions of the Earth's burgeoning population. It is conceivable that American interests in building New Cities around the world will prove a *trillion*-dollar industry.

Finally, think about what this might do for America's image around the world. What better international diplomacy can there be—for any country—than improving the cruel realities of poverty-stricken people around the globe, regardless of race, religion, or nationality, giving them better jobs and a stake in prosperity? How much better will that be than exporting bombs and war machines and destruction—or worse, supporting corrupt regimes that subjugate their own citizens and breed hatred of America?

And who better to accomplish this than America?

PART II –
WHAT WILL THE NEW CITY
LOOK LIKE?

Chapter 4 – Infrastructure: Making It Turnkey

It should be obvious to everyone that the primary, major advantage of building the New City from scratch will be the ability to proactively and precisely plan every single detail with respect to the layout and design and beyond—from critical services to cultural amenities to open space. This will be an intensive and exacting process—and probably a nerve-wracking one as well! It will require the best minds that America has to offer in urban planning, technological science, fabrication and construction, and human ergonomics on a broad, metropolis-wide scale. No doubt the very blueprints for the New City will be destined for enshrinement in the Smithsonian Museum in our national Capital!

In this chapter I want to talk about various essential aspects of urban infrastructure, and explore innovative ideas that will enable the New City to run like a fine Swiss watch!

Transportation

How will we most efficiently and most comfortably move people, including residents, out-of-town commuters, and tourists and visitors, around the New City? When you look at America's old, established cities, what do you see? On the East Coast, in places like New York and Boston, one sees incredible overcrowding and transportation infrastructure that is taxed to its maximum carrying capacity during every rush hour, every morning, and every evening. (In fact, "rush hour" is a serious misnomer—in most cities, east and west, it should be "*rush hours.*") Moreover, the cost of significantly improving the transportation in those old-line cities is simply staggering. For example, the Boston Central Artery/Tunnel Project, which came to be called "The Big Dig," ballooned from a projected cost of $2.8 billion to a mindboggling $14.8 billion by the time of its completion! And that is nothing to say about the massive disruption and years of traffic snarls and inconvenience that the prolonged construction of the tunnel created for millions of city residents, commuters, and, of course, business owners.

Out west, the endless, far-flung sprawl of cities like Los Angeles, Phoenix, and Dallas make the logistics of efficient and effective mass-transit systems utterly impractical, with any such efforts doomed to fail. It's no wonder that the music video of famous singer-songwriter Randy Newman's hit "I Love L.A." contains footage of the artist and his "girlfriend" driving around in an open, red, vintage Buick convertible the size of a yacht! If you want to get anywhere in L.A., you have to drive there. The more that both urban and suburban areas are allowed to spread out, the more impractical mass-transit systems become. Both of these extremes are object lessons in designing the right kind of integrated, people-moving transportation system to be implemented in the New City.

I envision a transportation design that borrows the best elements of traditional mass transit and combines it with new smart technology, but which also "downsizes"—or to use the term I prefer, which *modularizes*—the componential structure of the system, right down to the very vehicles that will run on it.

One thing that has always struck me whenever I have found myself using mass transit is the relative emptiness of many trains or buses during off-peak times. I must concede the fact that I do not regularly take mass transit; I live in a city and a region of the country that is, let's just say, underserved by these modes of public transport. So my experience is largely restricted to traveling on mass-transit systems in other cities at times of the day when ridership is light—but I mean *really* light! I cannot tell you how often I have climbed aboard a bus or a light-rail trolley only to find that I am one of three or four passengers scattered inside a huge cabin that is far larger than necessary at that particular time.

At the same time, I am sure that virtually everyone who has ever ridden public transportation during non-rush hours has had the experience of waiting for the next train or bus for what feels like an eternity. Now of course, it makes perfect sense that transportation authorities run fewer buses and trains during off-peak hours. It would be financially wasteful, not to mention downright irresponsible, for them to do otherwise. Actually, even the few off-peak vehicles that they do run are colossally wasteful, since only a handful of passengers ride the systems during the slow periods of the day or evening. Why not modularize these systems to make them smaller, more nimble, more intuitive?

What I have in mind is a radical new approach to a smart, surface transportation that is capable of being much more "pinpoint" in its capability to provide virtually individualized intra-city travel service to residents and visitors alike. To begin with, every street and thoroughfare in the New City will be embedded with GPS sensors linked to tracking software that will allow transportation controllers to oversee and monitor the movements of public-transit vehicles throughout the city. Let's be clear: In-street surface light-rail transit no longer requires the "rail." Computerized systems and sensing devices make it possible for transit vehicles to travel every street in the city —the entire urban grid becomes the rail line. Not only that, but sensors built into the cars can virtually guarantee the complete safety of the system by detecting approaching pedestrians or vehicles (cars, bicycles, whatever) and ordering the car to stop.

The transit vehicles themselves will be miniaturized; or rather, the city's fleet of light-rail cars will include a large contingent of small-capacity (six-to-eight-passenger) vehicles that can be rolled out during off-peak times. During the appropriate hours, these modular vehicles will be free-roaming—they will not be tied to any set transit schedule or to specific point-to-point travel routes. Instead, they will be able to be directed to any specific part of the New City that riders wish to go! Think about it! It's a Saturday, and you decide you want to do some shopping. You use your home computer or even your handheld device to summon a transit car, which arrives in front of your building as you walk out the door. You tell the vehicle to take you to the shopping district, and off you go!

In fact, much of this technology already exists, and New York City is already experimenting with a mobile "app" that allows users to "hail" a yellow cab using their cell phones or other hand-held devices. But here's an interesting obstacle: as it so often seems to be with all new innovations that are proposed in our existing cities and town, the program is mired in political in-fighting. Presently, the full implementation of the mobile app faces opposition from the Taxi and Limousine Commission (TLC). Presumably, once the TLC is satisfied that the mobile app is not detrimental in any way to their drivers—it would certainly seem that an application that makes it *easier* for people to hail a cab ought to be a great *benefit* to cab drivers trying to make a living—they will drop their opposition. However, that process may take years!

The great advantage of the New City is that we will be able to institute these kinds of people-convenient technology systems with getting mired in political battles between government and special interests. As I stress throughout this book, the New City will be built on the principal of minimal government involvement and thus minimal governmental regulation. Instead, the focus will be on the good of the people, in particular, those who will be living and working in the New City itself.

Thus, in essence, the New City will have the most user-friendly, modular, "smart-cab" surface public transportation in the world. And I think that we should come up with a really catchy name for these things! That could be another way to get our American inventors excited about doing what America does best—use our ingenuity to design and build new things. As far as a name goes, that might be another item for which we hold a national contest through which everyone can be involved, getting the whole country further excited about all of the great things that will go into creating the New City.

What would you want the name of the New City to be? Go to the website www.BuildTheNewCity.com and post your ideas!

During the high weekday commuter hours, of course, a large measure of the surface-transit system will be devoted to carrying workers to and from the business and manufacturing districts along regular routes and on established, regular schedules. Larger, higher capacity cars will be used, and more cars will be put into service. Belowground, the New City will have modern, high-volume metro-subway rail systems that will be designed to carry most of the commuting public to and from their jobs. But the key to the surface system will be flexibility—the ability of transport controllers to adjust the mix of transit vehicles out on the pavement—to maximize efficiency and minimize street traffic. The end result is that the surface system will in effect bring mass transit "closer" to users. It will create a kind of "on-demand" transit-service capability that will minimize wait times for those users at the same time that it minimizes the wasteful practice of running empty cars on rigid schedules that fail to serve the public in the first place.

During rush hours, the focus will be on the major belowground subway system designed to get people to and from their workplaces rapidly and efficiently. Metro stations will be conveniently located directly below, or near to, the major residential apartment buildings, condominium complexes, and single-family housing neighborhoods. I propose that there be at least one major rail station within a one-mile radius of each housing building or complex. The one-mile distance would encourage and allow residents to walk, thereby getting some exercise out of their commute to and from work without making the trek too difficult or too lengthy. Here again, an advantage of planning the precise layout of the New City in advance is the assurance that metro commuter routes directly align with residential, business, and retail districts. Finally, it is my hope that by strategically placing rail stations within walking distance of (but not too close to) residential buildings, perhaps we can encourage people, adults as well as schoolchildren, to get at least 30 minutes of brisk exercise a day. In that way, we can take a small step toward alleviating the increasingly alarming obesity problem that we have in the United States today. Just by making it convenient to walk to the train or light rail, we can encourage people to get some exercise!

Another inefficiency that I have observed in present-day transportation in our cities and towns is the overlapping, or duplication, of school-busing arrangements to an assortment of schools—elementary, high school, special needs, and so on. It's easy to understand how this evolved, with different school bus companies vying for contracts to accommodate both traditional student-transport needs and those necessitated by sports and other afterschool programs. And the duplication is often compounded by private schools. I see all this as a needlessly inefficient and economically wasteful way of getting kids to and from school.

In the New City, the efficiency and convenience of the mass-transit system will eliminate the need for separate busing for schools and students. Students from both public and parochial schools will be able to easily use the same systems as commuters and the general public. To the extent that it is feasible, school districts may be consolidated into centralized locations, although an emphasis must be placed on keeping most of those districts close to the residential areas where the students live, particularly for the younger, elementary-school-age children. Naturally, parents living in the New City will still want their children's schools to be nearby, and they will want their sons and daughters to be safe whenever they use mass transit. Thus, during school commuting hours, monitors will be employed to ride the buses and transit cars to supervise all of the children travelling to school, no matter what ages or grades they are in. By consolidating the transportation of all schoolchildren into the general mass-transit system, we should be able to hire fewer school monitors while achieving a high degree of safety for all of the children at the same time. And by consolidating school zones, and thus eliminating the redundancy caused by so many buses going to so many different zones, just think how much gridlock will be reduced, and how much fuel will be saved!

Along with all of this emphasis on seamlessly convenient mass transit, we must not overlook the opportunity of encouraging and providing the means for residents of the New City to get good and healthful exercise. Therefore, a network of bicycle paths also will be integral to the city's "floor plan," extending throughout the city through lanes and passages that are separate from the city street grid and motorized traffic. The bicycle-path system will be both above- and belowground, with the primary objective of safely bypassing intersections with street traffic and pedestrians.

And speaking about belowground, what about this idea? Think about a series of commuter-dedicated bike lanes that are weather-protected and temperature-controlled, either air-conditioned or heated as necessary, to enable workforce commuters to bike their way to work without being excessively overheated, sweaty, and exhausted?

Bicycle use will be strongly encouraged. For example, secure parking lots strictly for bicycles will be built below both residential and office buildings. The bike-lane system will be designed to accommodate larger, more stable pedal vehicles—let's call them carriages—that will be easier for elderly and physically challenged people to use. A limited number of both the bicycles and the carriages could be equipped with small, rechargeable electric motors powerful enough to move the vehicles through the bike lanes, but not so powerful as to turn the lanes into an amusement-park thrill ride! The electric motors on these vehicles could be solar-powered, but they would also be capable of being quickly recharged. Convenient recharging stations will be located at strategic points throughout the bike-path system, and users will be able to plug in whenever their bicycle or carriage is low on power.

Wherever the New City is built, more than likely the terrain will include some hilly areas that might pose difficulties for casual bicycle riders. Why not install large-scale escalators to assists riders on the steeper uphill grades? The "steps" of the escalators could be made large enough to accommodate the length of the average bicycle, and the escalators would be built alongside the regular bike path, giving cyclists the option to pedal up the hill on their own power or to comfortably and safely ride the escalator. We could entertain a variety of designs for these assist mechanisms, such as elevators or escalators, or perhaps build units modeled after ski lifts, like ski chairs, T-bars, or other devices (See Figure 2).

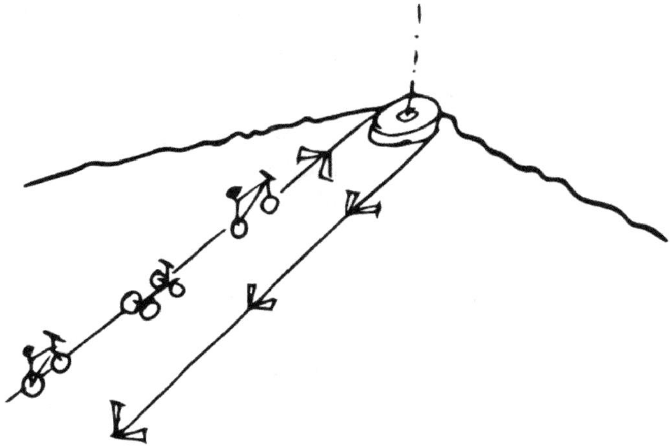

Figure 2. A simple bicycle lift for inclined bike paths.

Matching the bike-lane system will be an equally sophisticated network grid of pedestrian paths and boulevards in which the only wheeled vehicles allowed will be baby strollers and rolling walkers. Most of the pedestrian-path system will be aboveground and in the open—but, depending on the climate of the region where the New City is finally built, a component of it could conceivably be built underground, or may include long, aboveground stretches weather-protected by Plexiglas covers or enclosures that would provide year-round comfort and convenience. Of course, like the bike paths, the pedestrian system will effectively eliminate most street crossings where, in typical cities, walkers, cyclists, and motor vehicles meet. If you don't think such is important, consider this. In a recent report, the National Highway

Traffic Safety Administration (NHTSA) reported that in the year 2010, 4,280 pedestrians were killed on American roads and highways, stating that, "On average, a pedestrian was killed every two hours and injured every eight minutes in traffic crashes." That is certainly reason enough to keep cars, trucks, and buses separate from pedestrians—and to keep both of them separate from the bike paths!

If you have a vivid mental image of the New City as a metropolis in motion, with the working parts of all these various transportation systems whizzing around with incredible harmony, speed, and efficiency like electrons racing around a nucleus in an atom, than you have a good really good picture of how terrific I envision it will be. What's your vision for ideal systems for moving people around an ultramodern urban environment? Go to the website www.BuildTheNewCity.com and post your ideas!

Commercial Truck Traffic and Waste Removal

In many ways a city is like a living organism. It must be "fed," and a metropolitan population of a million or more people requires a constant, unending stream of heavy- and light-duty truck traffic delivering all manner of consumer goods to supermarkets, retailers, businesses, and shops around the clock, 24/7. At the same time, the average city today generates an incredible amount of waste materials that must also be disposed of efficiently on a daily basis. I want to discuss the waste-removal component first, because street sanitation is a major quality-of-life issue in just about every large American city.

Garbage trucks, or sanitation trucks as they are sometimes called, are omnipresent in our cities. They are big and bulky, and difficult to maneuver down and around the narrowest streets, some of which date back centuries to horse-and-buggy days. They are inherently dangerous, because their sheer size makes it difficult for their drivers to see small cars, bicycles, and pedestrians, and as a consequence they are involved in thousands of traffic accidents every year, including many that involve fatalities, quite sadly.

And let's be honest: They stink. Garbage is put out on city streets, awaiting pickup by sanitation crews. As it sits there, it attracts rats and other vermin; it breeds bacteria and becomes unhealthier by the minute; and it smells really bad. If you don't live in one of these major cities and don't think that garbage is that much of a quality-of-life issue for urbanites, think about how a prolonged garbage-worker strike that caused trash piles to grow into mountains along city streets was enough to end the tenure and political career of a popular mayor, one whose previous performance had been highly regarded—that is, before the strike and all that stinky refuse started piling up!

Of course, once the sanitation trucks pick up the garbage from the street, they haul it to a number of localized transfer stations, where all of the rubbish is consolidated and loaded onto huge, tractor-trailer-sized containers or open waste haulers to be trucked out of the city to incinerators or landfills—which are often hundreds of miles away. The location of these transfer stations is also a contentious issue with city residents who don't want such facilities in their neighborhoods. In addition to being dirty and smelly, transfer stations have a further detrimental effect on neighborhoods because they generate an immense amount of traffic from garbage trucks and big-rig haulers, as well as a tremendous degree of noise from both the vehicles and the plant machinery used to transport and load the refuse. It's pretty understandable why no one wants to live near a garbage-transfer facility. Thus, city officials and planners face incredible opposition whenever and wherever they propose putting a garbage-transfer station within city limits.

But there is an efficient and elegant solution to all of these problems, and it is a remarkably simple idea. It is called an Automatic-Vacuum Waste-Collection System, or a pneumatic-refuse collection, and such an arrangement is already being implemented in Songdo in Korea. And one of the interesting things about large-scale automatic-vacuum waste collection is that it is really not a new idea. The technology has been around since 1965, when the Swedish company Envac installed the first pneumatic-disposal system in a suburban residential district of Stockholm. Today there are nearly 1,000 such systems operating in over 30 countries around the world, including one servicing over 10,000 residents of Roosevelt Island, located in the middle of the East River in New York City. A massive, citywide pneumatic-disposal system is currently being installed in Songdo in South Korea.

The concept itself is very simple. Trash is placed by the residents into receptacles or loading stations that are strategically located around residential and office complexes. From there it is sucked through a series of steel pipes, sometimes traveling at speeds of 60 miles per hour, to a giant trash compactor where it is compressed to one-fifth of its original size, and trucked to an incinerator or landfill.

I envision that wherever it is practical, virtually all of the trash generated by the New City will be removed in this way. Imagine an entire city with no trash on the streets, no dangerous garbage trucks roaming the streets day and night, no battles in City Hall over where to locate garbage-transfer stations, and—most importantly—a cleaner, more enjoyable, and more peaceful living environment. Imagine what a beautiful environment that will create at street level, unlike the often gritty and unpleasant atmosphere that one finds in most major American cities today.

Recycling

But let's face it: the New City, just like any other, will have to deal with all of the larger items of trash that people generate. No matter how advanced our technology, appliances and equipment become obsolete, fail, or otherwise lose their usefulness, and dealing with bulk trash effectively must be a priority. As the most technologically advanced metropolis—and the "greenest" city—in the world, the New City must be a model of recycling innovation, effort, and technology, and that we should strive to achieve as clost to 100% recycling of discontinued-use articles as humanly practical. In fact, I propose that one of the first major industries that should be established in the city should be recycling—to the point

that the New City becomes known as the world's leader in
the field.

We can begin by becoming the foremost and largest
recycler of worn automobile and truck tires. According to
the website www.ridelust.com, Americans throw away 240
million tires every year, and of those fewer than 7 percent
are recycled—that leaves over 190 million worn tires that
pile up in landfills all across the country. However, using
existing technology, we can recycle virtually all of those
tires by using them to create Rubberized Asphalt Concrete
(RAC) that can be used to pave modern roads in the New
City and elsewhere across the country.

According to a report released by the Department of Civil
engineering at Clemson University (http://
www.clemson.edu/ces/arts/benefitsofRA.html), using RAC
to pave new highways or to resurface existing ones
beneficially uses between 500-2000 scrap tires per lane
mile! It also:

+ Reduces reflective cracking in asphalt overlays
+ Reduces maintenance costs
+ Improves resistance to cracking and rutting in new
pavements
+ Increases pavement life
+ Improves skid resistance
+ Decreases noise levels

Reduced costs in both construction and maintenance are
always a good thing, but when I think about the issues of
quality of life in the New City, I find the last item in that

list extremely attractive and exciting. The website
www.ridelust.com reported that using RAC to pave
highways reduces road noise by as much as a whopping
85%! If you have ever visited a major city in the U.S., you
well know how deafening the noise from traffic can be—
especially if you have ever tried to make a cell phone call
from street level. Granted, some of that noise is from
vehicle engines and blaring car horns, but just think about
what a terrific achievement it would be if we could reduce
the very significant road noise component by 85%. The
ridelust website concludes that using rubberized asphalt
concrete "makes for better roads, that's an established fact.
We have a surplus of old tires in this country wasting away
in our landfills, and we have roads that are constantly being
worked on and in need of repairs. The obvious conclusion
is to use those waste tires in our roads."

Recycling represents a unique niche for innovative ideas
because the solutions that people come up with absolutely
do not have to be high tech in nature. Recycling of worn
automobile and truck tires is just such, very simple idea.
We see ordinary, everyday people come up with novel and
even inspired uses for everyday discarded items—
everything from the most practical to the most sublime, as
some artists create sculptures from machine parts or other
scrap. The point is that it is really up to one's imagination.
Do you have any ideas about how we can effectively
recycle the materials of our modern age? Go to the website
www.BuildTheNewCity.com to post and share your ideas!

As I mentioned at the beginning of this section, the
"organism" of the city must also be fed. Just as trash must

continually and constantly be removed from a large city, a relentless stream of consumer products and raw materials must be brought in. At the same time, different goods that are produced by businesses and manufacturers within the city must be shipped out to customers around the world. A significant part of the economic vitality of the New City will depend on fast and effective commerce.

What I envision for the product-delivery and -distribution functions in the New City is a bit like the trash-removal system in reverse. The New City will be surrounded by as many package-processing facilities as needed to efficiently deliver incoming products to businesses, retailers, restaurants, and residents throughout all of its districts. These processing centers will receive the bulk shipments from over-the-road trucks or rail services. They will then break down the shipments for pinpoint delivery to the correct recipients in the city proper. One option for achieving this that should be carefully considered is a system of secure conveyer-belt mechanisms that carry the products right to the subbasements of business and residential complexes for them to be offloaded and delivered. Barcode matching will be used to guarantee that products are delivered precisely to their intended recipients. I imagine an arrangement a little bit like the best intentions of the famous conveyer-belt system that was designed for handling passenger baggage at the new Denver International Airport—but with the bugs worked out, of course! The important aspect is that all of these delivery systems will share the same infrastructural system to eliminate the costly and inefficient redundancy that we have in our cities today.

In addition, an underground light-rail system using the same principles could also be employed, and perhaps the ideal situation will be to have a conveyer-belt setup alongside the light-rail network. Such a system will require very careful planning to ensure it has failsafe emergency capabilities while at the same time avoiding the same kinds of redundancies we have at present. Finally, goods that are shipped out of the city will of course be transported from within the city proper to the perimeter distribution centers and from there forwarded to their ultimate destinations. The net result, and of course the goal in all of this, will be a significant reduction in the amount of large and small trucks rumbling over city streets. This includes in particular heavy tractor-trailer rigs, but also the types of box trucks that are typically used by overnight package-delivery companies like UPS and Federal Express.

And here's a question: How many times have you seen multiple express-delivery trucks from different companies all show up at the same building at the same time? Sometimes two or more trucks from the *same* company, just delivering to different businesses in the same building? It's a shameful waste, even if it is something that (seemingly) can't be avoided in present-day cities.

Now imagine all of those trucks gone from the street, and *all* of the packages delivered to *all* of the companies in a business complex (or to all of the residents in an apartment complex) by a single conveyer or light-rail system that eliminates the endless circle of duplication of truck after truck delivering packages to different individuals, over and over again.

And it should be pointed out, since one of the concerns of the New City is job creation, that this internal system of package and product distribution is not intended to put the delivery companies out of business. Keep in mind that those companies will still serve a vital role in getting products to and from the perimeter processing and distribution centers. In fact, the within-city distribution system should actually make things easier, cheaper, and more efficient for those companies because their drivers will not have to waste time driving around city streets in heavy traffic searching for delivery addresses and jockeying for space in loading zones (or tying up parking spaces). In addition, paying the fees at toll bridges and tunnels to get in and out of the New City will be eliminated for these carriers.

Finally, it is important that we be practical here. It is entirely possible, perhaps probable, that some limited commercial-truck traffic will need to have access to the inner districts of the New City on a regular basis. It may turn out to be the case, for example, that fresh foods and critical medical supplies will need to be brought directly to markets and hospitals over city streets. Special accommodations for the swift, direct delivery of perishable goods and emergency or life-saving medications may have to be carefully designed into the overall development plan. But the point of all of these transportation ideas and innovations is to achieve a *dramatic*—make that a *radical*

—reduction in the overall volume of motor-vehicle traffic on the streets of the New City. It will result in a safer city with cleaner air, less congestion, and a more peaceful and enjoyable environment for city dwellers and visitors alike. So what do we do about privately owned vehicles?

Private Cars in the New City

It always seems that any discussion about the future of the privately owned family car inevitably begins by talking about the hallowed and storied place of the automobile in American culture. We hear about how Americans love their cars and the freedom of the open road, and the automobile is often painted as the symbol of that autonomy. Our love affair with the automobile is documented and celebrated in hundreds of movies and television shows; we have car clubs devoted to our favorite and most iconic models, like Corvettes and T-Birds. For many Americans, perhaps nothing else generates as much "pride of ownership" as that polished, four-wheeled beauty in the garage. Personally, I can relate, because I too have a great love for the automobile, and one of my great passions and hobbies is racecar driving, which is something of a hobby of mine.

In thinking about the New City, I believe it would be a fantastic achievement if the mass-transit system I have described would be so efficient and so user-responsive to residents that no one living within the city limits would ever need to own a personal automobile. How terrific would it be if the readily available transportation options in the city were so seamless that anyone could get anywhere simply by stepping out the door and jumping onto a light-rail or subway connection and being whisked to their destination?

However, I am the first to concede that this is an idealized picture. As wonderful as it sounds, particularly to those of us who are environmentally conscious, I believe that we must be realistic and practical about the need to accommodate personal automobiles in the New City. I will not belabor (or argue with) the perfectly valid point that some Americans will not want to give up their beloved cars. (I am probably one of them!) On the other hand, I believe that some amazing things can happen when mass-transit systems are so masterfully designed to meet the commuting and travel needs of city residents that owning a car simply becomes unnecessary.

Ultimately, I do not believe that such a well-configured metropolis is particularly far-fetched. I think that anything is achievable if we put our minds and hearts to it. The point is this: Let's allow ourselves—let's *challenge* ourselves to dream and to build those dreams into a reality! Let's dare to be great!

In fact, it is just as much a matter of practicality when people begin to realize that their ownership of a car represents more of a burden than a convenience, particularly when they have a highly convenient mass-transit system at their disposal. For residents of any given city, owning a car is of course most obviously a financial burden, but it is also a practical one: Finding parking is difficult (and can also be expensive); the poor condition of the roads in many of our cities inflicts tremendous wear and tear on our cars, resulting in high maintenance and repair costs; and so on. Gasoline prices in most major cities tend to be higher than they are in the suburbs or in rural areas. Unfortunately, in some city neighborhoods, car theft and vandalism are major concerns. Let's face it: All things considered, for all of the advantages of owning a car, there are also a lot of headaches that come along with it, particularly in a city environment. But I firmly believe that something can be done about these issues in the New City.

It is interesting to note that according to a 2011 report from the Federal Highway Administration's Office of Highway Policy Administration, the state with the lowest percentage of licensed drivers per residents is New York State—an amazingly meager figure of 59%. That means that 41% of New York State residents *do not own a driver's license.* (Data from: fhwa.dot.gov/policyinformation/pubs/hf/pl11028/chapter4.cfm) Of course, if you think about that statistic a little bit, you might say, "Obviously, since New York City has one of the largest subway systems in the world." Furthermore, anyone who has ever navigated the streets of Manhattan by car or on foot certainly has a vivid memory of thousands of careening taxicabs and limos for hire. So of course, the greatest concentration of people who do not possess driver's licenses is in New York City.

But think about this: New York is a fairly large state by area, and there are vast suburban and rural areas where owning a car is more or less a necessity. With eight million people, New York City represents about 42% of the state's 19 million residents. If, as I've said, the greatest concentration of people who do not own driver's licenses is in New York City, the percentage must be staggering—probably in the area of 75 to 80%, and that may be a conservative estimate. Keep in mind that while New York City does have a terrific mass-transit system that is highly reliable and for the most part dependable, it is not without its problems. It is an old system that routinely experiences operational delays due to breakdowns, construction and repair, and weather-related situations. But millions of people depend on it.

Now imagine an ultramodern transit system, created with the benefit of strategic preplanning having been built into the very blueprint of the New City, which is able to run at 99% efficiency and on-time performance. If New York City is able to function and its residents to prosper with upwards of 80% of those inhabitants not owning driver's licenses, what percentage might we achieve with the New City? Ninety percent? Ninety-five percent? The prospects are very intriguing and exciting. And there is certainly good reason to be hopeful: There are interesting indications that younger generations of Americans may very well be ready and willing to reverse the trend of automobile dependence as the primary or preferred mode of travel, particularly in urbanized areas of the country.

America's Car Culture in Transition

Most of the evidence comes from several recent studies that show that fewer young Americans are getting driver's licenses. In the United States, social-science researchers have noted the general trend that, from about 1983 to the present, the percentage of Americans with driver's licenses has slowly declined for every age group under 50. However, in recent years this decline among younger people has become significant. In one study, using data from the Federal Highway Administration and the U.S. Census Bureau, Sivak and Schoettle (2012a) found that the percentage of persons 19 years old who had driver's licenses dropped from 87.3% in 1983 to 69.5% in 2010. For 17-year-olds, the percentage went from 69% in 1983 to an amazing 50% by 2008.

There are a multitude of factors that may play a part in this significant decline. Certainly the harsh recession over the past five years is a likely one. Add to that the price of gasoline—if you can't find a decent job, you certainly can't afford to be tooling around town wasting gas at $4.00 per gallon or higher. And of course, like everything else, cars are always getting progressively more expensive as well. With more and more kids coming out of college with tremendous debt from their student loans, monies they need to start repaying in short order, it certainly makes no sense to add to that already onerous burden by buying a car and incurring additional monthly payments. The data bear this out. According to CNW Marketing Research, Americans between the ages of 21 to 34 purchased 38% of new cars in 1985, but only 27% of them in 2010 (Sivak & Schoettle, 2012a).

Some critics point to other factors as being at least partially responsible for the decline of young people both getting driver's licenses and buying fewer cars. They cite restrictive limitations imposed by many states on teen driver's licenses that take the "fun" out of using a car for many young people. Restrictions include a driving curfew; a limit on how many other teenagers may be in a car with a teen driver at the wheel; and the swift suspension of driving privileges for moving violations like speeding or careless driving. As one online commentator put it, "If you can't drive at all after dark when you're under 18 (as is the case in some states), or you must have a parent with you, what fun is that? The only thing for which you can use the car for is to go to work—and that's only if you can find a job."

Critics also cite the high cost of insurance imposed on young drivers, even when they are added to their parents' existing policies. And some even blame part of the decline on "helicopter parents"—overprotective parents who are so fearful for their kids' safety that they won't let their children anywhere near the steering wheel of the family car, much less buy their own vehicle.

However, restrictive licenses and high insurance costs in the U.S. do not explain the worldwide trend toward fewer young people obtaining driver's licenses. In another study, Sivak and Schoettle (2012b) researched driver's-license data in 15 countries and found similar trends in seven of them: Sweden, Norway, Great Britain, Germany, Japan, South Korea, and Canada. The researchers noted that these countries have several characteristics in common, and particularly important among them are that they are all wealthy nations in which a high percentage of the population lives in very large cities. Now, keep in mind that recent census data in the United States also indicate that young adults are gravitating to our larger cities—reversing yet another time-honored trend of flight to the suburbs. But here is where it gets really interesting. Because another common factor across all of these countries, one certainly applicable to the U.S. as well, is the large percentage of their populations using the Internet.

Sivak and Schoettle suggest that there is strong evidence that teenagers and young adults are replacing "road trips" with social networking and other Internet usage as a means of connecting with and keeping in touch with their friends. Gloria Bergquist, vice president of the Alliance of Automobile Manufacturers, says, "For generations, the automobile has typified freedom. At 16, many people wanted to get their driver's license because that was the way people connected with their friends. [Today] we're seeing people connect through their iPhones. That's their primary motivation—to be in touch with their friends." As another online commenter put it, with all of the expenses and hassles of having a driver's license and owning a car, not to mention the traffic in most of our cities, "Social media just makes it so much easier to connect with friends via cellphones, texts, face time on Skype, Facebook, and all the rest."

Not only that, the ability to shop online means that teens and young adults no longer need to go out to malls to buy the things they need or want. Who wants to fight the traffic when you can order just about anything from the comfort of your living room (while you are perhaps Tweeting with your friends)? In a 2008 article exploring the decline in automobile sales to young people in Japan, the *Wall Street Journal* reported, "Having grown up with the Internet, they no longer depend on a car for shopping, entertainment, and socializing, and prefer to spend their money in other ways."

If you look at all of these trends together, is isn't difficult to see how all of this bodes well for the viability and success of the New City project, and also why I believe the New City will be an extremely attractive place for many people (younger Americans in particular) to want to live. As discussed elsewhere in this book, the entire New City will be equipped with ambient intelligence in all of the homes, businesses, offices, workplaces, retail shops, and open spaces like city streets and parks. The ability to communicate via the Internet will be omnipresent; "connecting" with one's friends will be as simple as breathing.

Furthermore, the sophisticated and people-responsive— people-interactive, really—transit network will also make it easier to meet up with one's friends at any given time in any given part of the city. No need to hold a driver's license; no need to buy a hugely expensive automobile and pay the ungodly insurance premiums that come with it; and no need to store and maintain that vehicle. Thus to a large extent and for many people of many different ages, the sophistication and structure of the New City will nearly uniformly make car ownership (and dependence) obsolete for its residents, and even for tourists or other visitors. Furthermore, thanks to highly efficient mass transit and sophisticated, instantaneous, and highly accessible communications systems, the cost of living in the New City will actually be lower for young people, but also for older residents as well.

I began this section about private cars and their place vis-à-vis the New City with a note of practicality, and I would like to end it with one. Having one's own car will always be important to some people. In the New City, some residents will want to own a car to be able to travel outside the city or to other parts of the country. We can easily accommodate this need by building garages or safe parking lots at strategic places on the outer city limits, similar to the way long-term parking lots at many U.S. airports operate. And I believe that people should know how to drive—you never know when you might have to take the wheel in the face of an emergency. Perhaps one modest goal we can achieve is this: by providing all of these safe, comfortable, affordable, and convenient modes of travel, we will be able to turn the residents of the New City into "one car families" instead of the situation that seems most prevalent today, that of the "two-car family.

Finally, one other option that might be made available in the New City is some variation of the "Zipcar" concept that has become very popular in a number of U.S. cities. Zipcar members can reserve a car for personal use for any time of the day or night for a couple of hours or the entire day, on a regular or irregular basis. It's like a timeshare for a car; and since some companies include gas and insurance costs in their flat rate, some of the most negative aspects of owning a car are eliminated. An added benefit of this concept is that car-sharing companies are very keen to attract environmentally conscious customers by building fleets of hybrid fuel and electric vehicles that get terrific gas mileage while minimizing toxic emissions. Obviously, this

Build the New City

fits in very well with the Green Cities concept that is at the heart of the New City ideal. Given these benefits, I can easily see such a concept working very well within the New City's transportation-network matrix.

How much do you depend on your car, and how strong is your desire to own one? What if you lived in a vibrant technopolis like the New City, which provided virtually all of your intra-city transportation needs? Post your thoughts on the website at www.BuildTheNewCity.com .

Chapter 5 - Power and Water

I firmly believe that America has to get serious in its discussions regarding power in the 21st century, and the inevitable role that nuclear energy must play in fulfilling our long-term power needs.

The New City will include the construction of a new, dedicated nuclear-power plant. In brainstorming radical, highly efficient ways to meet the city's electrical-power needs, I considered building small nuclear-power plants in strategic locations primarily on the outskirts of the city but within easy reach of the people who would operate these mini power stations. I have had to rethink that idea, because I realize that such a plan may present a real nightmare for homeland security, which of course would have to then protect all of these discrete units from acts of terrorism. Not a pretty picture. I still think that nuclear scientists and technologists might take a closer look at this idea if security analysts think that they can find ways to overcome the considerable security challenges that it poses.

In any case, I think that a nuclear plant specifically dedicated to providing electrical power for all of the New City's immediate needs must be built. But it must be one that has the full capacity to meet the power needs of the city for at least 25 years into the future, accounting for whatever expansion will occur over that time.

I have talked about many of the distinct advantages of building the New City from scratch, but the most significant one lies in the choosing of the perfect site upon which to build this dedicated nuclear-power plant. Despite the fact that there are presently 104 nuclear-power plants in operation throughout the United States, Americans remain rather nervous about nuclear energy. In a 2011 survey conducted shortly after the Fukushima Daiichi meltdown disaster in Japan, CBS News concluded that public support for building new nuclear-power plants in the U.S. had dropped to 43% (Michael Cooper (March 22, 2011), "Nuclear Power Loses Support in New Poll," *The New York Times*). On the East Coast, the memory of the accident at Three Mile Island in Pennsylvania is still amazingly fresh on people's minds. So for the New City, once the optimal site for the urban center itself is chosen, determining the optimal location for the power plant will be a critical step.

We must choose as wisely as possible, and based on the best scientific data we can generate. We need ground that is exceptionally geographically sound and away from serious fault lines, but near enough to water sources that are adequate (or better) for cooling the reactors. Starting from scratch will enable us to site the nuclear plant at a relatively safe distance from the city itself, minimizing the impact of any plant emergency situations upon the city. Naturally, we hope that such situations will never occur, but we must anticipate such possibilities and be prepared to do whatever is necessary to deal with them effectively.

It stands to reason that the best place for the power plant will be some distance outside the city limits. It will be connected to the city via separate metro-subway lines whose use will be restricted to the engineers and workers who will operate it. These restricted transit lines will be equipped with high-security checkpoints to prevent unauthorized persons from gaining access to the plant. In fact, it should be noted that all of the major infrastructure facilities, industrial-manufacturing plants or factories, and transportation hubs that will be located on the perimeter of the New City, perhaps even just outside of it, will be similarly connected to the inner city by high-speed subway-rail lines. This includes the power plant; water-pumping stations; solid-waste transfer installations; water-treatment plants; heavy manufacturing and industry; and, finally, the airport and train stations.

While traditional nuclear-power critics have valid concerns, I believe that nuclear power must be a component of the New City. We must first do everything we can to make nuclear power as safe as humanly and technologically possible. Then we must resolve our philosophical differences on this issue as best we can to everyone's satisfaction.

Earlier I said that the power plant must meet the immediate electricity requirements of the New City plus having the capacity to meet the city's needs for at least 25 years out. However, it is important to note that the main power plant will not be the sole supplier of electrical energy for the city. I believe that it will be vitally important to exploit every opportunity for generating power that our scientific research and innovative technology makes possible. I also believe that many of these efficient systems can be built right into the very structure and form of the buildings and parks of the New City itself, mostly in ways that are so unobtrusive that neither residents nor tourists will even notice that they are there, humming away, producing power from sun, wind, and water.

To begin with, the rooftops of all of the major buildings in the city will be equipped with arrays of either solar panels or micro wind turbines, or perhaps both, depending on which of these technologies is best suited to specific buildings. Solar panels can be built right into the structural "skin" of the glass and steel high-rise office and commercial buildings and made to look just like the windows. For residential buildings, it might make sense to place the array of solar panels on the roof.

Another technology that will be used extensively in the New City will be micro wind turbines. Obviously the giant, windmill-style turbines that one sometimes sees in rural wind farms or in offshore installations are impractical for use in urban applications. For one thing, they are just too big and obtrusive; they also produce vibrations and other noise that would rattle nearby windows, disturbing nearby residents or businesses.

The solution to harnessing wind power in the New City lies in microturbines that can be strategically installed on the roof levels of major buildings to take advantage of the unusual and sometimes unpredictable wind patterns that tend to happen in major cities with a lot of high-rise buildings. The buildings often form canyons through which airflow is channeled, sometimes at different speeds and different directions depending on the prevailing weather conditions. Micro wind turbines are versatile enough to use the quirky patterns of big-city winds, such as turbulence and wind shift, to continuously and efficiently generate power for the residential or commercial buildings on which they sit.

The efficiency must be applied to the water systems as well. The New City will require billions of gallons of clean, potable water, and it will also generate a tremendous volume of wastewater. Why not also use these two water-delivery and -removal systems to generate more electrical power for the city?

Pumped-hydro storage is a power-generating technology that is already in use (and has been for decades) in many places across the United States. Here's how it works: The typical pumped-storage plant consists of two reservoirs, one at an upper elevation and the other at a lower elevation. These are connected by a huge pipeline or penstock that runs through the pumping/generating station on the lower reservoir level. Located in the pumping/generating station, which is essentially the powerhouse of the whole complex, are one or more reversible pump-turbines.

These units act as pumps when operated in one direction and as electricity-generating turbines when operated in the other. Combined with each of the reversible pump-turbines on the same shaft are reversible motor-generators that, along with the pump-turbines, act as motors in one direction and as generators in the other. During off-peak hours, when electricity usage is low (usually at night), the electric company usually employs surplus power from its conventional high-efficiency generating stations such as hydroelectric dams or nuclear-power plants (See Figure 3).

During peak electrical usage, the water is released from the upper reservoir down through the penstock and back to the lower reservoir, moving the pump-turbine, which turns the motor generator (now working *as* a generator) to produce electricity. There is a certain irony in there being a significant loss of energy between the pumping and generating cycles such that it generally takes three kilowatt-hours of pumping to produce two kilowatt-hours of generation. That means that the pumped-hydro storage system actually loses more power than it creates! However, the low cost of the power used during off-peak hours in the pumping operation is more than offset by the much higher price that the electric company charges its customers for power during peak hours of operation, thus making the pumped-storage power plant economically feasible. pumping operation is more than offset by the much higher price that the electric company charges its customers for power during peak hours of operation, thus making the pumped-storage power plant economically feasible.

You are probably thinking that by today's standards, pumped-hydro storage is pretty low-tech and unexciting. However, I believe that in really looking closely, one has to be impressed by its elegant simplicity; and as I've stressed throughout this book, I firmly believe that we must apply all of the innovative and technological resources that

Figure 3:
Pumped Hydro Electricity Generation

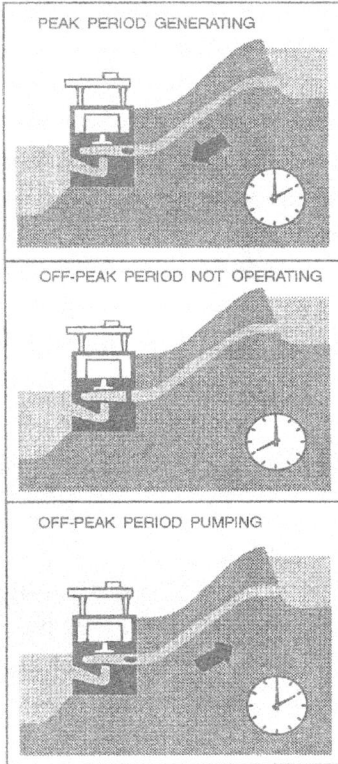

we can to making the New City as energy efficient as possible, no matter how unglamorous they may be. The fact that a relatively ancient technology can still be effective in an ultramodern technopolis is actually rather remarkable; and if you consider the fact that all pumped storage really does is take advantage of the forces of nature—water and gravity—you suddenly realize how much that approach is in keeping with the natural, harmonic spirit and organically driven environment of the New City. Imaging the idea of an urban metropolis that is in harmony with the natural environment and does not needlessly stress that environment.

In fact, the developers of Tatu City in Kenya have demonstrated the high value that can be obtained from low-tech solutions that are exquisitely simply and satisfyingly intuitive. For example, all of the warm-water heating will be provided by solar power (Nairobi is only 90 miles from the Equator, so of course there will always be plenty of sunlight), and there will be no air conditioning allowed anywhere in Tatu City.

You have to be exclaiming, "Ninety miles from the Equator and no A/C?" But that is indeed correct. Instead, Tatu City will employ a low-tech alternative cooling scheme that has been in use in Africa for over a decade. All of the buildings will be equipped with chiller rooms built into the basements. The rooms will freeze large packs of ice overnight during off-peak hours when electricity use is low. Then, during the day, large fans will continually blow an uninterrupted stream of air over the icepacks that keep the building cool. The system is expected to save a massive 40% on electricity costs throughout the entire city.

I believe that the most important lesson that we should take away from these examples—and one that we should keep firmly in mind when we build the American New City —is the need to be open to all ideas and concepts that might serve to improve our end result, whether they come from cutting-edge computer or telecommunications technology, or simply from a new twist on an old idea, like Tatu City's giant-icebox formula!

Do you have ideas about how to generate energy, or about ways to use electrical power more efficiently? Go to the website www.BuildTheNewCity.com and post your ideas!

As a further example, with respect to the potable water that the municipal authority must bring into the city, we can install turbines in each of the underground aqueducts that carry the water, and then use those turbines to generate electricity. And unlike the pumped-storage station just described, it may even be economical to generate power with those turbines during peak-usage hours. That is, one would imagine that the best time to run the turbines would be during the heaviest water use by the city itself; conceivably, this would be when the greatest volume of water would be moving through the aqueducts to city users. Conversely, if there are times during low water usage at which it is not economical to run the turbines, they could be shut off or bypassed by rerouting the water supply through separate pipes not connected to the turbines.

At the wastewater end of the system, water that has been treated and cleaned could be pumped into a reservoir situated at a higher elevation than the wastewater-treatment plant, and stored. From there it could be released downhill during the hours of peak energy demand and used to turn the turbines and generators of a power station before it is returned and effectively recycled, presumably to a large river or lake. In this way, all of the hydrological resources of the New City can be used to augment its needs for electrical power.

There are a couple of difficulties with current pumped-hydro storage stations, not least of which is that they are very expensive to build. This is especially true on a small scale, which is how most such stations in the U.S. have been built. However, I believe that the cost factor will be less of an issue given the fact that one or more pumped-storage power plants can be incorporated into the overall master plan for the New City. In selecting the final site on which to build the city, it may be necessary, at least in part, to look for topographical features that will make pumped storage power stations feasible.

Land topography is also an issue because, according to Michael Totty (2011), "Current technology generally requires a large 'drop,' or change in elevation, to produce much power." Totty goes on to report that power companies "are working on lower-flow hydro turbines that can work in more level settings." Certainly, if such low-flow turbines can be produced, they will be ideal power-generation machines for use in the New City. Here again, we need ideas. We need people in technological and scientific fields to study these problems, and people in the building and construction fields familiar with the physical logistics of such systems to brainstorm solutions—but I also believe that we all can contribute ways to make pumped hydro more efficient. And again, I encourage readers to go to the "Build the New City!" website and post your ideas there. As you can see, these solutions to not necessarily have to be "high tech"; they can be based on ancient wisdom and knowledge of basic physical systems, either on their own or in combination with new and emerging technologies. Let's start a discussion to solve this.

In the end, the "exciting" part of this old-fashioned and perhaps "mundane" water and gravity technology will be its full integration into the virtually unseen workings of the infrastructure—just like the solar panels and micro wind turbines on the roofs of the buildings, or even the electronic ambient intelligence that will be built into every people-space in the New City. How amazing it will be that 21st-century digital technology will operate side by side with that of the ancient Romans!

Chapter 6 - Smart Homes, Smart City, Smart People

Clearly one of the most exciting and fascinating features of the New City will be the intensive application of "smart" computer and sensory technology that will be built into the very infrastructure. One of the fastest-growing areas of computer technology and its applications is ambient intelligence (AmI). AmI is an amalgam of several multidisciplinary areas of research directed toward providing very significant, and potentially pervasive, benefits to individuals and society in general. The basic idea behind AmI is that by combining and coordinating microcomputer technologies and devices with highly sophisticated sensors within a given environment, "a system can be built to make decisions to benefit the users of that environment based on real-time information gathered and historical data accumulated" (Augusto & McCullagh, 2007).

What that means in everyday language is that home-installed AmI systems will be able to "learn" the needs and habits of residents, and adapt by actually making decisions for those residents for their ease and comfort. For example, that might mean switching on the lights in a home office at the usual time you go to work, or automatically turning up the heat in your family room in the evening when you typically sit down to relax and read or watch television. Now, that's a very simple example, but it is a parlor trick compared to the very real and very beneficial capabilities and efficiencies that will be achieved through the carefully designed application of AmI—not just in homes and offices, but throughout all the public areas of the New City. Functioning as more than a simple convenience here and there, AmI will not only make daily life easier for millions of people, some of its applications will actually save lives.

This chapter covers the truly remarkable advantages and benefits that AmI will bring to residents of, workers in, and visitors to the New City. To gain some perspective on this new technology, it may be useful and revealing to talk a little bit about what our homes are generally like today; specifically, to discuss the kinds of rudimentary "smart technology" that most of us actually use right now.

You're probably asking, "What smart technology?" But the fact on the matter is that most of us live in homes or apartments that were considered "smart" by 1960s or 1970s technological standards. Think about it: We have thermostats that we use to control the climate in our homes, most with multiple heating zones that can be set independently to different temperatures. We have clock radios that can be programmed to turn on or sound an alarm to wake us up in the morning; and in our kitchens, most of our appliances are equipped with control timers to set cooking duration or to switch on at a predetermined time; and so on. We put lights on timers for security, and our garages are equipped with automatic door openers.

Over the decades, we have added other such automated conveniences: Answering machines to receive messages, smoke and carbon-monoxide detectors, and TV remote controllers that we can fight over! More importantly, people with serious medical conditions wear life-alert devices that they can easily activate in case of an emergency. Today most new homes have sophisticated, built-in home-security systems that can be programmed to our individual needs, and which are linked to monitoring stations that immediately notify police in the event of a home invasion or break-in. Our cars are similarly equipped with antitheft devices.

All of these innovations are examples of smart technology, even if we generally do not tend to think of them as such. In a way, that is actually one of the hallmarks of smart technology—we are not truly cognitively aware that it is "working" for us. It is akin to someone happily using the telephone to talk with a friend 3,000 miles across the country while conceding, "I have no idea how or why the phone works." We are all glad that it does, however. If we look closely, though, there are at least two drawbacks to this generation of 20th-century smart technology.

The first is that, for the most part, none of these systems exist beyond their primary function, or are integrated with any of the other smart systems; they all function independently. Thus, the thermostat controls the heat quite separately from the oven timer that controls the cooking time, which in turn is quite separate from the security system that "patrols" the perimeter of the house. The second drawback is that in order to actually function as designed, virtually all of these discrete systems require action on the part of the homeowner or resident. Thermostats and timers must be each individually set, radio alarm clocks tuned and security systems programmed.

Messages received on the answering machine or in voicemail go no further—they are essentially "canned" on the device until the recipient keys in to listen to them. Garage-door openers require the push of a button—even something as critical as the emergency shutoff for the furnace requires someone to physically get to the switch and flip it.

Finally, another problematic issue with a number of these separate devices is powering them up. Things like smoke and carbon-monoxide detectors require batteries—lots of batteries—to keep them functioning properly at all times. Here again, it is up to the home or business owner to constantly replace the batteries, as public-service announcements at the beginning and conclusion of daylight savings time endlessly remind us to do. In order to be truly integrated, a smart system should provide for the uninterrupted delivery of power to all components of the unit; or, at a minimum, it should be capable of notifying the homeowner when specific devices require battery replacement.

To be sure, these are, or were, all great conveniences, but . . .

What all of this points to are the truly remarkable, game-changing differences between the smart technology of the 20th century and that of the 21st century. Let's first tackle the issue of the integration of smart technologies into a single, interconnected, intelligent master system that through a kind of actual "knowledge transfer" promotes the globalization of technology to all parts of the entity. In plain words, the underlying necessity is for all of these systems to "talk to each other."

The Realization of Ambient Intelligence (AmI)

We can trace the route that got us to where we are today, and that we are traveling toward the actualization of AmI, by following up the previous discussion of 20th-century smart technology with a brief look at the rise of computer technology—and more particularly, at computer use by the general public.

To begin with, few new technologies have undergone a more rapid and pervasive transformation during their first decades of existence than computer science and artificial intelligence (AI) science. Moreover, perhaps no new science has ever engendered higher expectations, nor possesses higher potential for creating and deploying technology to improve our daily lives and the ways our created environments can be designed to help us. The computer and digital revolution in the last two decades of the 20th century essentially expanded upon the existing smart technology that I just described. In the 1980s many companies had one or two computers—say, one for billing and accounting, the other for information processing, business letters, and such—that served separate functions, were not "linked" in any way, and thus could not "talk" or communicate with each other, even though they were in the same office.

I do not need to go at length here into how the Internet changed all of that. But briefly stated, many offices began internally by connecting their growing numbers of in-house computers into intranet networks through a mainframe computer that served all aspects of the company and enabled informational communication across all centralized computer terminals. With the creation of the Internet, the potential for networked communication and worldwide interconnection simply exploded (which hardly seems a powerful enough word to describe it), as we have seen with email; various social media; and the seemingly endless opportunities, platforms, and tools for instantaneous information-sharing and data transfer.

But that isn't even the half of it, because the digital revolution has by no means been limited to homes and offices and computers. Instead, the miniaturization of microprocessors and the prodigious, almost incalculable mega-geometric increases in computing power have allowed us to take "pieces" of smart technology with us wherever we go. Thus, when we travel outside the home, we stay in touch via mobile phones and PDAs. In our cars or on foot, handheld GPS navigation devices help us successfully get to our destinations. Computer chips implanted in our pets that become lost allow perfect strangers to identify the owners and (hopefully!) contact us to arrange the return of our beloved animals. And a growing number of those life-alert devices for people with medical conditions now provide access to critical medical and treatment histories that can be critical if, say, the wearer becomes ill in a different city far from home and their personal doctor. The applications of digital technology appear to be endless. As Cook, Augusto, and Jakkula (2007) state, "Computers that perform faster computation with reduced power and tailor the computation to accomplish very specific tasks are gradually spreading through almost every level of our society." I would replace the word "gradually" with "rapidly," and delete the word "almost"!

In any case, the pervasiveness of these computer-based systems and the idea of interconnecting them all into a vast user-friendly, universally interactive interface are what underlie the whole concept of ambient intelligence, and they are the driving forces behind making it a reality. As Augusto and McCullagh (2007) point out, "Networks, Human Computer Interaction (HCI), Pervasive Ubiquitous Computing, and Artificial Intelligence (AI) are all relevant and interrelated but none of them conceptually covers the full scope of AmI. Ambient Intelligence puts together all these resources to provide flexible and intelligent services to users acting in their environment." In a word, the goal of ambient intelligence on the "intelligence" side (at least part of the intelligence side, as we will see later) is to have all of these intelligent networks "talking" to each other and working together to provide useful information to the user. We get a primordial glimpse of this targeted information sharing—and information *routing*—when, for example, we click on a particular website, perhaps out of mere curiosity with no intention of buying anything, only to find later that advertisements for the products we viewed are showing up on our computer screens and mobile devices. (Not, perhaps, the most desirable use of information sharing and routing!)

The "Disappearing Computer"

But it is the second, rather fantastic component that distinguishes and elevates ambient-intelligent technology above all of the smart, computer-based systems that have preceded it, precisely because it represents the integration and coordination of all of the previous science into a single, coordinated "brain"—if I may be so bold as to use that term. In effect, the computational and electronic advances of the past decade have exponentially increased the level of autonomous and quasi-intelligent behavior that interconnected smart systems are capable of producing. As we will see, this capability has already been successfully built into experimental smart homes; and indeed, it is now being integrated into smart-city projects like Songdo and Tatu City. Cook et al. (2007) state that the promise of ambient-intelligent systems is that:

> By enriching an environment with technology (e.g., sensors and devices through a network), a system can be built such that acts as an "electronic butler," which senses features of the users and their environment, then reasons about the accumulated data, and finally selects actions to take that will benefit the users in the environment (p. 3).

In other words, smart-home ambient-intelligent systems gather data on the activities of the inhabitants of that home, and they "learn" from that data. They see the occupants' behavioral patterns, proclivities, preferences, and daily habits through repetitive action; and then through a kind of reasoning, the ambient system acts *on its own* to adjust the environment to the needs and wishes of those residents. Here again, imagine an ambient-intelligence system that, after deducing that you generally go into your family room at 9pm to relax and watch a little television before going to bed, turns up the heat and flips on the light—and the TV—before you get there.

This feature of self-acting responsiveness and decision-making by ambient-intelligent systems achieves a distinct transparency that aligns with the notion of the "disappearing computer," a term that may have been coined by the late Mark Weiser, who has also been called "the father of ubiquitous computing" by those in the industry. In his paper *The Computer for the 21st Century*, Weiser wrote, "The most profound technologies are those that disappear. They weave themselves into the fabric of everyday life until they are indistinguishable from it."

Incredibly, Weiser wrote that back in 1991! The term "ubiquitous" is defined as "present, appearing, or found everywhere." But what Weiser meant is that not only will ambient computing be everywhere, it will be so pervasive that no one will notice its presence—at least not in any conscious, cognitive way. Like those telephones (and wireless and cell phones or PDAs) that are indeed everywhere, but which we now seldom notice. (Most of us *still* don't know how they work, either!) In the smart homes, offices, and other spaces of the New City, ambient-intelligent systems will be everywhere, making life easier or more comfortable for the people that live and work there. We won't even be cognizant that they are helping us behind the scenes.

It's like Pinocchio after he becomes a real boy. Bear with me for the sake of analogy: Pinocchio is still an automaton, of course, but the strings are gone! But enough about theory—let's take a look at some real-life examples of what is and may be possible to achieve through the implementation of ambient-intelligent, computer-networked systems.

Ambient Intelligence in Action

Ideally, the truly smart home in the New City will be one in which virtually all of the functions, appliances, and artifacts are enriched with a combination of wired and wireless remote sensors that enable the ambient-intelligent system to gather information about their use, as well as about the activities of users in the home. This includes the home heating and cooling systems; all of the major devices in the kitchen and elsewhere (ovens, stoves and microwaves, refrigerators and freezers, and the clothing washer and drier); the lights and window shades; and even small items such as coffeemakers or other countertop appliances. AmI would also monitor sensors embedded in the furniture, particularly chairs, sofas, and beds, through which it will be able to detect when any of these items are in use. In short, the smart home will collect usage data on just about everything in the house, as well as the behavioral patterns of each inhabitant.

Then, through a process known in the computer world as "data mining," the smart home will analyze all of this collected information and use it to make autonomous decisions and initiate actions that benefit the home's inhabitants—ultimately without those users even being aware that these actions have occurred. The endgame of the smart-home concept is the creation of an intelligent dwelling that behaves or operates as a rational agent and makes decisions based on predicted values that are obtained through the analysis of all of that usage data. What that means in very basic terms is that the smart home learns your daily routine, and begins to perform some of the functions therein for you.

But, in all likelihood, one of the greatest benefits of smart systems in the homes and offices of the New City will be the many ways that smart environments will protect the health, lives, and safety of human users. Cook et al. (2007) point out that the myriad features of intelligent environments will soon pervade our entire lives, automating aspects of our everyday existence, increasing work productivity, customizing our shopping habits and experiences, and even reducing wasteful practices with regard to water resources and electrical-power consumption. However, they begin by citing the very significant amount of research that is presently being conducted into finding ways that AmI and intelligent environments can (and indeed, must) be created and designed to help with health monitoring and assistance. Next, these authors point to health-care services becoming decentralized from large hospital and convalescent facilities toward more community- and home-based health-care capabilities. More than just a matter of large hospitals and insurance conglomerates wanting desperately to save money, this trend truly reflects "the importance that

Americans place on wanting to remain in their current residence as long as possible" (Cook et al., 2007, p. 19).

Given these trends and people preferences, Cook et al. (2007) argue that there is "tremendous need for research on ambient intelligence to support the quality of life for individuals with disabilities and to promote aging in place." They add that there is a critical financial incentive: "By 2040, 23% of the population will be 65+, and over 11 million people will suffer from dementia from Alzheimer's disease, with the long-term projected total losses to the U.S. economy expected to be nearly 2 trillion dollars." And finally, "Given the costs of U.S. nursing homecare (approximately $40,000 a year with an additional $197 billion of free care . . . by family members) . . . use of technology to enable individuals with cognitive or physical disabilities to remain in their homes longer may be more cost effective and promote a better quality of life" (p. 19). Rather than "may be," I believe that to be a categorical and undeniable fact.

Education

Ambient intelligence will not only bring tremendous benefits to the educational system within the New City, it will serve to enhance the learning experience for all students. And it will do one more thing that is sorely needed in our country: make education much more egalitarian and universal.

Today many schools are using various forms of smart systems for teaching and instruction. For example, many elementary and high schools use interactive "whiteboards" on which teachers and students can write or draw and have that same information appear on the virtual tablets or laptops that students are using at their desks, or in use elsewhere in the classroom. On the college level, more and more "e-universities" are being established, and many of them are becoming more accepted in the traditional academic community, albeit very slowly. Nevertheless, I believe it will just be a matter of time before, at minimum, the most academically rigorous of these e-universities gain full acceptance and accreditation in the scholarly and academic world. While some of the students "attending" e-universities never see the inside of a classroom, a surprising number of them set up onsite at existing brick-and-mortar colleges or universities that they are required to attend, usually for a week or more, several times per semester or during the academic year. I very much like this model as one to be instituted in the New City. Thus, on the one hand, we have computer-based AI technology being used as a kind of educational "intranet"—within the confines of individual schools—through the interaction of electronic whiteboards and other devices. On the other hand, we have remote, home-based educational capabilities thanks to home computers; students can readily connect with schools and institutions via the Internet (not to mention the rich and limitless research resources that are available via the World Wide Web). My vision for a universal system of education in the New City is to marry all of these valuable features into a cohesive and interconnected system.

However, I want to begin by addressing the issue of egalitarianism as mentioned briefly at the beginning of this section. Far too often in our country, the best interactive technological devices for educational instruction—such as touchscreen boards and student laptops or tablets (along with other advanced equipment)—have only been available to those living in affluent cities, towns, and communities, or those who can afford to send their children to private, magnet, or special charter schools. In so many poorer school districts that cannot afford these marvelous, technologically advanced tools, the students must do without, and their parents have little choice in the matter. The disparity in educational opportunity that this situation creates and perpetrates is profound and disturbing, and I believe it is simply wrong on every level.

I believe that the New City will be the great equalizer when it comes to providing quality education across the entire spectrum of students—from the children of lower-income families right up to the wealthy. I absolutely do not want to sound like a politician when I say this, but one of the most important things that we can achieve, for today's children and for those to come—and as an investment in the future of our nation—is to restore America's ability to give all children equal opportunity to receive the best education in the world.

First, of course, creating the city from the ground up will give us the rare and perhaps unprecedented opportunity to build all new and modern schools, utilizing the kinds of techniques, architecture, and layout plans that will ascertain which available environments are the most appropriate for classrooms, lecture halls, laboratories, athletic and recreational facilities, and other in-school spaces. At the college level, this will of course also apply to dormitories and other living spaces for students.

I believe that far too often, we have been guilty of building schools on the cheap. The reason is obvious. Under our present system, whenever a new school needs to be built, or an existing one expanded because of population growth, it is the people of the particular town (or a wider sending district of multiple towns) who must pay for it— usually themselves, without any outside help from county, state, or federal governments, and certainly without corporate funding. How often do we read about school districts that reject referendums for new buildings or expansions? The answer, of course, is, "All the time!" The skyrocketing costs of construction materials and labor over the past few decades have made it impossible for many local districts to build and maintain adequate schools.

What I propose for the New City is that the building of the schools should be made part of the overall financing partnership of the corporations and industries that will create it, but with some of the funding also coming from municipal bonds that will be offered as a means by which every American (and others, too!) can invest in the city and make a little money at the same time (see Chapter 8 on financing the New City). I further propose that we accept nothing less than the building of schools designed to last at least 50 years, not ones with the meager 20-to-30-year lifespan new educational facilities may reach today. By creating superior structures from the outset, we can possibly circumvent the cost-cutting tendency— understandable as it may be—of local school districts to build substandard or scaled-down new facilities that are often inadequate for future needs.

Next, like all of the homes and offices in the city, all of the schools will be enriched with ambient intelligence with a particular focus on strategies and features that enhance the educational process and experience for teachers and students alike. I have already mentioned teacher- (and student-) controlled electronic whiteboards communicating with handheld devices students use at their desks. Research is being conducted into technology that can turn an entire classroom into an interactive tool. One of the first such experiments is KidsRoom at MIT (Bobick et al., 1999, cited in Cook et al., 2007). KidsRoom is a virtual-reality space much like the flight simulators airlines use to train commercial pilots in which students are immersed in an adventure and must work together to accomplish tasks or explore a story. In doing so, they learn math, language, and other important skills. For example, the task might be that the students must navigate a boat on a river to a specific location upstream. They have to use mathematics to calculate how much gasoline they will need for the miles they travel; compute the time it will take based on wind current and speed; use geography to chart their course (avoiding rapids and shallows); and so on. Only through teamwork and task completion are they able to advance the story to the next project. In short, the whole classroom becomes part of the lesson.

Ubiquitous AmI in homes and schools also makes it possible for students to participate in their classroom lessons remotely. Now, I want to be careful and clear about this aspect of education as it pertains to elementary and high-school students. Some people might view AmI as a great way to make it possible for all children in the New City to, in effect, to be homeschooled. I do not advocate this at all. I believe that the socialization that occurs in a positive educational environment is critical for the development of children into mature, respectful adults. Stated bluntly, in the best of worlds, in which school facilities are designed and built to the highest educational standards, I believe that the benefit to children of being together in school classrooms and settings is immeasurable. Indeed, that is the very reason that earlier in this section I called for the building of the best, most sophisticated and learning-conducive school environments that we can imagine and make into a reality. Hands-on teacher involvement and interaction is also critical to the learning and socialization processes. If I didn't believe in the importance of socialization in school classrooms for children, and close teacher involvement, we could simply save the money, not build any schools at all, and homeschool everyone on whiteboards using AmI. I believe that is a very bad idea.

However, there may be times when it will be extremely convenient and practical to use the AmI in students' homes as an adjunct to in-classroom instruction. For example, we can easily imagine weather conditions occasionally being an issue. Depending on where the New City is built, events like occasional snowstorms or even hurricanes might make it too dangerous for kids to travel to school. Classes could be conducted remotely by the teacher for all students (although I concede that the kids will be none too happy to realize that they may never have a "snow day" off from school ever again!). One can also imagine a periodic, temporary situation in which class size might become an issue due to a spike in the number of school-age children in a certain grade. With AmI in everyone's home, it will be possible to have most of the students attend their classes in school, while others participate from home—the student body rotating so that all of the students get equal and adequate classroom-instruction time. And finally, another potential use for AmI in the home might be for students who are occasionally absent from school due to illness or other circumstances to get their lessons for their missed classes remotely, and thus keep up with the rest of the class. This flexibility, adaptability, and accessibility will enable the New City educational system to be truly universal by giving every student the very best opportunities, as well as providing safeguards to make sure that pupils requiring remedial help will get it from both teachers and parents. The phrase "No child left behind" will go from a political platitude to an educational reality. If you have ideas about how AmI might be used to promote and improve teaching practices and learning opportunities, post them on the website www.BuildTheNewCity.com.

Training Centers, Job Boards, and the New City Website

While all of that may sound wonderful, I believe that the emphasis on education must not stop there. Too often in America we have this notion that, once you get that high-school diploma or college degree, and a skill set for a particular occupation, you are "trained up" for life and your education is essentially over, except perhaps for occasional, minor on-the-job training as the situation warrants. That may have been largely true earlier in our history. But if the digital revolution and the rise of the information age have taught us anything, it's that the workplace of today, and of the future, is a dynamic mosaic of change in which things are accomplished in new ways with new tools. The need for continuing education to keep up with the latest developments is crucial to one's success.

From time to time during our current recession, in which the nation's unemployment rate has seemed to be permanently stuck above eight percent, we have heard the refrain from employers that they cannot find the skilled workers that they need to fill their jobs. These employers point to what they call a "skills gap" as playing a significant role in prolonging the economic downturn, and more critically, as a primary reason why American companies are not hiring. A number of CEOs for these companies have been quick to lay the blame for this supposed shortfall on our educational system for not doing enough to prepare individuals with the knowledge and skills they will need to successfully join the workplace.

However, in a recent online article in *Time Business* (http://business.time.com/2012/06/04/the-skills-gap-myth-why-companies-cant-find-good-people), Peter Cappelli, Professor of Management and Director of Wharton's Center for Human Resources, calls the skills gap "a myth." Cappelli charges that companies seem to "want experienced candidates who can contribute immediately with no training or startup time." As evidence, Cappelli cites a 2011

Accenture survey that found that "only 21% of U.S. employers had received any employer-provided formal training in the past five years." Clearly, there is a serious disconnect here, with companies complaining that they cannot find qualified applicants to hire, but at the same time refusing to provide much in the way of training to new hires. In his book *Why Good People Can't Get Jobs*, published in June 2012, Cappelli argues that it is not a skills gap that American businesses and workers face, but rather a "training gap."

I do not wish to get into a debate over who is responsible for this situation, but I wholeheartedly agree that there is currently a training gap in America that must be addressed if we are ever going to improve our unemployment picture. I am a firm believer that learning doesn't and shouldn't end with a diploma or college degree, but must be ongoing throughout our lives. I therefore propose that we build and create training centers throughout the New City for the sole purpose of getting workers "up to speed" with the knowledge or skills specifically required by the available jobs. For example, as the city is being built, if more design engineers or technicians are needed, training centers will immediately offer courses to people who will then be able to step right into those positions and make the kinds of immediate contributions that companies want. The same approach will apply for all of the other job opportunities in the city, from financial accountants to managers to customer-service operators to line workers to the complete gamut of tradespeople and laborers.

From there, if more specific on-the-job training is necessary, the various training platforms can hand off the individuals who successfully complete their programs to apprenticeships with specific companies operating within the New City. It should be possible for everyone in the city who wants specific occupational training to get it (provided that there are open, applicable positions), and conversely for companies looking to hire for specific jobs to enlist training centers so that the need can be met quickly with qualified, fully trained candidates. Such a broad-based network of training programs will make it possible to fill important job vacancies quickly, and it will also foster upward mobility among the people in the workforce able to take advantage of the training opportunities to learn higher-paying job skills and then be placed in those more advanced positions as the need arises. Furthermore, it will serve to connect job seekers with employers who have positions that need to be filled.

I envision a comprehensive and interactive job board utilizing the city's AmI computer network, which will enable individuals and employers to see extensive listings of the open training programs and available positions. Also featured will be possible future openings that companies feel *may* become available soon, so that people may be proactive in managing and upgrading their career paths. Thus, a person seeking a particular kind of work can immediately find out if there are currently job opportunities available in a given field; and, if so, where he or she can sign up for a training program if further education is necessary. On the other hand, if an employer needs to fill a particular position, he or she can consult the training-programs section of the website to find out what specific courses are currently being taught and when fully trained graduates of that program will be available for hire. And all of these parties will be able to keep track of what is going on in the New City's jobs market—what the trends are, and where promising future opportunities exist.

The New City job board must be viewable everywhere so that all Americans can log on to see what training programs, jobs, or other opportunities are available and apply for them accordingly. I have stressed throughout this book that the New City is a project by Americans for Americans, and that should include all Americans. I firmly believe that one of the keys to the success of the city, and to really getting the job done, will be soliciting the very best talent that America has to offer. In order to do this effectively, the New City information board must list not only available training programs and job openings, but also the growing city's large-scale needs for building materials, major construction projects, manufactured goods, technical services, and other equipment.

Not Just Jobs: Materials, Machines, and Equipment

Particularly critical in the construction phase will be the need to coordinate the massive amounts of materials, machines, and equipment necessary to build it, particularly given the short, 10-year timeframe for which we must strive in order to really jumpstart our still-flagging economy. City planners and developers will be able to use the materials-and-equipment section of the city's interactive board to post their building needs, whether it's steel rebar and structural concrete or computer/digital supplies and fiber-optic cable. Aggressive companies around the nation will be able to review these postings and respond with competitive bids to fulfill the city's various needs on the specific schedules that are required by the planners and developers. The winning bidders will profit from becoming partners in the building of the city. In this way, by regularly consulting the city's interactive board, people and companies across the nation will be able to participate in one way or another—whether actually or inspirationally—in the rapid process of building the city. The New City interactive board will be very much like a virtual report card, or the box score on last night's ballgame. People around the country will get up in the morning and check out the progress of the city over their morning coffee.

In sum, it is my hope that education will be an integral and vital part of the New City, and from the very start something that will be ingrained into its culture. Schools, universities, and learning and training centers will all complement each other to offer as many educational opportunities as possible to people, and not simply for job preparation or placement, but for the arts and music as well. At the same time, training programs and continuing-education courses will enable a broader and more efficient use of modern interactive school buildings, as these structures can double as learning centers during off-school hours. The result will be an atmosphere in which continuing education is valued, and to some extent rewarded through career advancement, upward mobility, and cultural appreciation. I believe it would be simply terrific if the New City came to be known as an "Education City" the way that some towns in the U.S. today have come to be known as "college towns" owing to the big universities in their midst, where the college and the town support and nurture each other. Can you think of anything that would have a greater impact in providing the highest possible quality of life within a city than having limitless educational opportunities and a vibrant cultural environment, including theater, museums, and the arts? I certainly can't!

Chapter 7 - Designing the New City: The DurantHybrid

Urban Design in the 19th and 20th Centuries

While attempts have periodically been made to design and create completely planned cities, most American cities have instead grown or expanded organically in response to burgeoning populations whose economic growth and prosperity created greater demands for housing, industry, commerce, and infrastructure. Unfortunately, the term "organically" in this context does not have the same positive aspect that it does when one is talking about organically grown foods that are free of chemicals, hormones and pesticides. Rather, organic growth in this case means that most cities expanded as a kind of after-the-fact response to rapid population and industrial growth, rather than having the opportunity or foresight to anticipate and thus plan for such evolution. As a result, urban planners have rarely if ever had the opportunity to predesign whole cities in advance, with an eye toward such concerns as operational efficiency and the logical layout of residential, commercial, industrial, transportation, and other elements. In most cases, cities simply expanded outward in all directions until coming up against barriers like rivers or mountains. The introduction of the automobile led to the expansion of inner-city-type environments (or what I call add-ons), ultimately morphing into what we commonly call "suburban sprawl."

I am not at all criticizing the architects and urban planners of the 19th and 20th centuries. When you look at the rapid growth of our country and the industriousness of our people, it is easy to see why perhaps no one could have imagined the explosion of growth that our cities would be forced to undergo, in similarly rapid fashion, without much time for logical planning and prudent or methodical urban design and development. For example, between 1821 and 1855, the population of New York City nearly quadrupled! Just how does one plan for that? You need a new factory— you find the land and you build it, hoping that the infrastructure will be adequate, or at minimum, that the logistical framework needed to get your workers to and from work will develop on its own. You need new apartment buildings to house the people, you find the land and you build it. And if all of that means pushing the "city limits" out farther and farther, so be it.

Still, there have been brilliances created by remarkable visionaries, such as New York City's magnificent Central Park, to name but one. With the conclusion of World War II and the recognition of the potential rise of other nations with global power came the sobering realization that the nation might one day have to defend its own borders. That gave rise to the Dwight D. Eisenhower National System of Interstate and Defense Highways—which we mostly just refer to as "the interstate" today. People can criticize the interstate all they want (Journalist Charles Kuralt, beloved for his "On the Road" segments on CBS-TV, is famous for having remarked, "Interstate highways allow you to drive coast to coast without seeing anything"), but the blunt fact is the interstate is a remarkable achievement in infrastructure construction that as of 2010 comprised over

47,000 miles of high-speed roadway. The interstate-highway system is yet another terrific example of Americans seeing a need and an opportunity, and rising to the challenge with a positive response that created jobs and a magnificent, modern network, helping the general population with new transportation resources that drastically increased our mobility and grew our distant and previously unconnected cities.

However, even planned cities in America have had their problems. Our own national capital, Washington, D.C., commissioned in 1790, is certainly majestic and gracefully pleasing to look at as you walk through the National Mall amid all of the monuments. By law, the city's skyline is low and sprawling, with a height restriction that prevents structures from being built any taller than the width of adjacent streets plus 20 feet. It is certainly well laid out and aesthetically beautiful. Yet city leaders have long criticized the height restriction, citing it as the main reason for Washington's urban sprawl, and which has also spawned an affordable-housing crisis and huge traffic problems. While the city Metro system has helped the situation since opening in 1976, it too is now overburdened as the second-busiest rapid-transit system in the United States, right behind the New York City subway. So, the bottom line is that even with our best efforts toward effective urban planning to advance and optimize urban life, we have fallen somewhat short, both aesthetically and operationally.

I believe that with foresight and diligent planning, and based on what we have learned in the past—plus a firm vision of where technological innovation is taking us—the design and creation of the New City will drastically change all of that. I want to begin with a brief overview of the basics of city planning. Actually, it's pretty simple.

The most common basic network or scheme that has been used to organize and develop urban space for convenient habitation is the basic "grid" pattern, and it dates back to around 2000 BC. As you might surmise, the grid is a basic pattern of geometric, square blocks characterized by streets at right angles and by the potential for unconstrained expandability—until one bumps up against a river or other formidable geographic feature. Historians surmise that the preponderance of the grid pattern can be explained by the tendency of city residents—both people and horses—to walk in straight lines, and thus the waffle-iron layout of urban street planning seems to have sufficed and served quite durably for nearly 4,000 years. Why change when you got it right to begin with?

The Radburn and the Fused Grid

And in fact, the only change that seems to have been developed in all of that time is what has come to be called the "Radburn" after the small suburban community in New Jersey where it was first implemented. What was the impetus for this radical new street design? The car, of course! The Radburn was designed in 1929, roughly 30 years after the invention of the internal combustion engine–powered automobile. Anticipating the coming dominance of the automobile as the vehicle of choice for people to get around, the Radburn community was billed as "a town for the motor age." The design sought to separate the modes of traffic with pedestrian pathways that do not cross and major roads at grade. It also employed a kind of nested hierarchy of pleasantly curving roads amid green space, but in which not all streets were "through streets"—the convenience the automobile provided meant that highways no longer were required to intersect or interconnect with every other highway, as "the shortest distance between two points" was no longer a concern to the modern, 20th-century motorist. (One should also bear in mind that the average price of gasoline in 1929 was 21 cents per gallon!) In so doing, the Radburn nested-hierarchy design also pioneered the use of cul-de-sacs, with pedestrian paths running through the green space and interconnecting the neighborhoods (see Figure 4).

Figure 4: The Radburn Street Network (Source: Wikipedia)

The next innovation in urban street planning took a lot less than 4,000 years to be created. However, it was little more than an attempt to combine the best elements of the grid and Radburn designs into a single cohesive system, one that is efficient and safe with respect to transportation facilities and needs, while at the same time being people friendly and aesthetically pleasing. In brief, the primary benefits of the grid design are generally seen as the reduction of travel distances due to lesser frequency of intersections; easy accommodation of mass-transit options (both above and below ground); and more "intuition" in making the laying out of the city (and the expansion of it) a relatively simple matter of squared blocks and plots. Navigating around a city with a grid-based design is a simple matter, even for a first-time visitor. In my view, the main benefits of the Radburn design can summarized as the creation of a more pastoral living and working environment. Some city planners argue that the Radburn design is cheaper to construct and maintain, but my impression is that a Radburn requires more real estate, and you are really just spreading the development over a wider area with accommodations for green space—although all of that is definitely good. The Radburn provides flexibility to take advantage of topographical features of the land, making it generally more picturesque, and giving local neighborhoods a more pleasant, sociable ambiance that may be especially beneficial to families with children. Finally, one of the most important advantages of the Radburn design, and one that I have already talked about and which will be an integral feature of the New City (see the section in Chapter 4 on Transportation), is that it is safer for cars, pedestrians, and bicyclists.

In any case, the synthesis of the ancient grid and the modern Radburn urban-street-network pattern is called the Fused Grid, and it was first proposed in 2002. The Fused Grid model creates a large-scale pattern of higher-travel, moderate-speed automotive and/or truck traffic that provides easy mobility and access to neighborhoods (whether residential, business, retail, etc., as the case may be). This overarching road grid in turn forms "precincts"— or neighborhoods, let's call them—within which the best elements of Radburn road design are used; and crescent-shaped streets, cul-de-sacs, and significant allowances for green and open space are also extensively employed. Furthermore, pedestrian and bike-path systems within these neighborhoods are designed to connect with and provide easy access to parks and public transit, as well as community and educational institutions (schools), retail establishments—even some governmental offices and businesses. The nested hierarchy of the greater connector-road grid system thus preserves the ability of the local precincts or neighborhoods to function without having through-streets that would otherwise encourage more automotive traffic, endangering residents and others within each local community (see Figure 5).

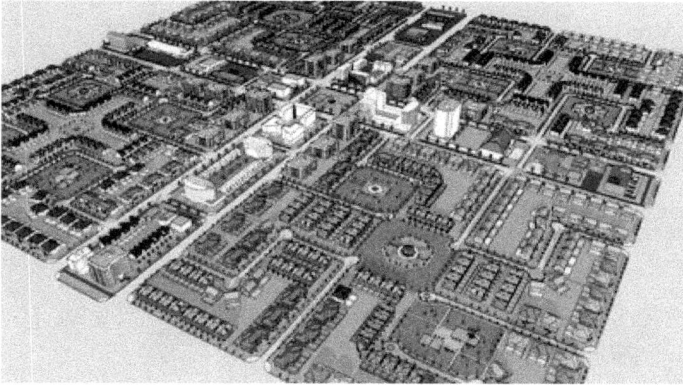

Figure 5: Fused Grid showing four neighborhoods with
twin connector roads (Source: Wikipedia)

In sum, the Fused Grid achieves three major benefits and
goals for pragmatic but people-sensitive urban planning:
(1) Easy navigability of the network structure; (2) A
significant level of safety at road intersections (of which
there will be far fewer) by reducing the volume of interface
between modes of traffic (automotive, pedestrian, and
bicycle); and (3) Connectivity through the linked network
of local, low-volume streets, connector roads, and bicycle
and pedestrian pathways (see Figure 6). I would add an
additional side benefit: The Fused Grid design gives people
the opportunity to walk more, thereby encouraging them to
get additional physical exercise.

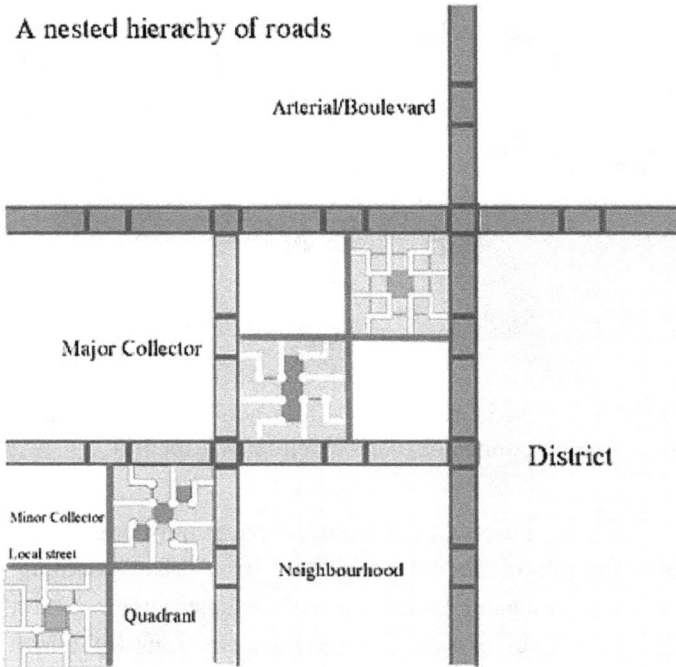

Figure 6: Typical Hierarchy of Roads in a Fused Grid
Transportation Network (Source: Wikipedia)

Finally, the nested hierarchy of roads in the Fused Grid network system naturally takes the higher volume of traffic and, at a certain level, transfers it to an alternative path. Thus, unlike a river that gets wider as it flows downstream (collecting more runoff as it goes), in the Fused Grid, automotive traffic emanating from the various local neighborhoods is routed to connector streets of ever-greater capacity—presumably topping out on the interstate system (just to complete the full progression to easy egress from the city).

Introducing the DurantHybrid

There is much to like about the Fused Grid model for urban transportation and neighborhood planning, although it is probably too soon to tell how effective it will ultimately be, given that it was proposed a mere ten years ago, and so far has been implemented in only two Canadian cities—Stratford, Ontario in 2004 and Calgary, Alberta in 2006—where its impact is still being studied and analyzed.

But I believe that the Fused Grid model can immediately be improved by adding another dual dimension to it— specifically, on the one hand, by factoring in the vertical dimension of allowable building heights across the entire spectrum of the New City skyline from the inner city to the outer-city limits and on the other, by allowing developers more freedom with permitted building and usage configurations (i.e., less zoning and building code restrictions) to create much more varied, multiple-use applications within each individual Fused Grid zone. In my view, doing so adds flexibility and diversity in creative zoning for the usages—be they residential, business, retail, or others—that the various individual fused sub-grids are allowed to offer. It also enables those different use zones to be distributed more evenly around the master grid, rather than being restricted to or concentrated in one district, as was the case in many American cities over the last two centuries (and to some extent still is today). (Indeed, even today New York City can be "partitioned" by the purpose-driven district names from an earlier era: the Garment District, the Diamond District, the Meatpacking District, etc.)

Let's begin by looking at the basic "floor plan" blueprint for the New City as displayed in Figure 7.

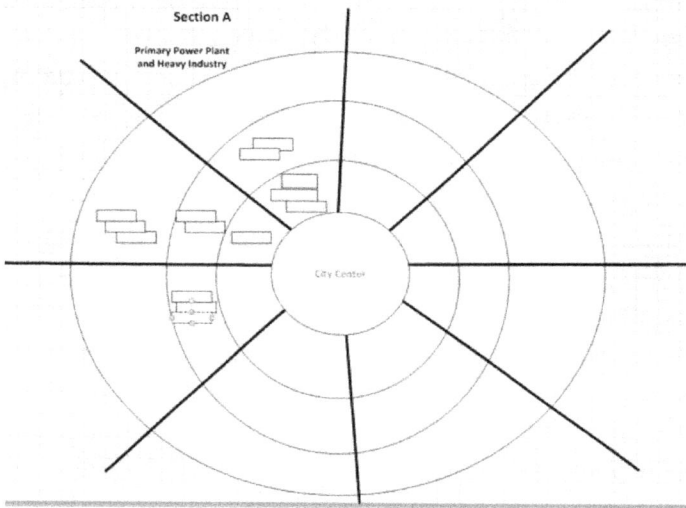

Figure 7: New City Basic Blueprint Map

As you can see, the design consists of four roughly concentric circles or rings at increasing distance from center city intersected by eight main "spokes" radiating out from the city center all the way to the outer borders. The city as a whole will essentially comprise a giant Fused Grid, and the spokes and rings of the basic layout will neatly, effectively divide the entire city into 32 smaller and separate—but fully integrated—Fused Grids. The spokes represent the primary transportation corridors that will include mass-transit rail, light rail, and conventional highways for automobile and truck traffic. Other modes of transportation will be reserved to those areas away from the main corridors with the goal of keeping motorized and human-power transportation separate for the safety of everyone concerned. Lastly, in the event of a city-wide emergency, the primary transportation corridors will make evacuations of all or part of the city both transparently simple for people to understand and easy for authorities to accomplish, since they will provide eight direct and rapid routes out. These primary corridors will also be the main conduits for managers and workers commuting to and from work at the heavy-industries, manufacturing, power, water, recycling, and trash-removal installations, as well as commercial-air and -rail hubs, which will all be grouped on the outer perimeter of the New City. We've already reviewed one key attribute of the DurantHybrid—the idea that heavy-industry, transportation, and utilities installations are to be located on the city perimeter. In this way, we place the noisier (and smellier, with respect to garbage consolidation and removal) building complexes away from residential areas (See Figure 8)

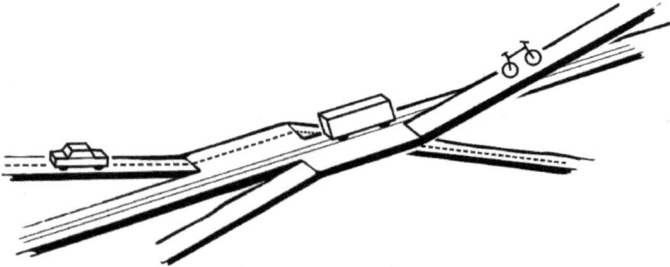

Figure 8: DurantHybrid multi-use transportation artery.

Another attribute that I think we must look at is what I call high-volume, low-frequency parking synergy. We might be able to take advantage of these synergies to reduce the need for massive parking lots at places like stadiums, churches, and schools. Let me give you an example: In Texas, where I live, and across much of the Midwestern and Western U.S., there are huge churches and temples, at each of which hundreds of thousands of people congregate every Sunday, packing massive parking lots with thousands of vehicles—for one day, or for a few hours of one day. The rest of the week, those lots are empty. Considering the aforementioned need and desire of people to hold onto the personal or family car, is there some way we can group or consolidated certain facilities such that the necessary evil of parking lots for personal cars and light trucks (forgive that "necessary evil" terminology—I've already acknowledged in the transportation chapter that we recognize the need and desire of people to hold onto the personal or family car) can be reduced somewhat? With respect to churches and temples, it might not be wise to group them with stadiums or major-league ballparks, since Sunday is also Game Day in the NFL as well as other sports. But what about schools that are generally open from Monday to Friday and idle on weekends? I believe that a well-thought-out plan wherein we group together such high-volume, low-frequency institutions or facilities may reduce the required size of parking lots in the New City by as much as one third.

The next attributes of the DurantHybrid that I want to discuss are the "soft-transportation" linkages and usage-varieties for each of the 32 Fused Grid city zones. By "soft transportation," I mean primarily pedestrian and bicycle linkages whereby people may move easily from one zone to other without encountering too many interfaces with the connector roads that carry motorized traffic. This is a feature taken directly from the Radburn design, but I want to advance it a step further. Because I envision each (or most) of the 32 zones—neighborhoods, really—having a limited but adequate amount of retail and service businesses, such as grocery stores, salons, home-goods and -improvement shops, professional-service providers, and so on, such that the people living in each neighborhood do not have to go very far to obtain the basic necessities to live comfortably in their neighborhoods. At most, they should have to go no farther than say, to an adjoining zone or neighborhood, and ideally, most able-bodied residents should be able to walk there.

Additionally, with proper preplanning and foresight, each of the 32 neighborhood zones can be built independently— think of them as separate but interconnected modules—and on different schedules as needed as we rapidly construct and populate the city sector by sector. It is here that we must learn a lesson from Songdo City. One of the primary, fundamental reasons universally cited for the current and continuing success of Songdo (where previous attempts to build such complete and technologically advanced new cities have failed) is the groundbreaking decision (no pun intended!) by Songdo's developers to build the residential and commercial-support infrastructure first—before all the gleaming, ultra-futuristic office towers started to go up. After all, the people who are going to work in those magnificent office towers need a place to live; they need schools for their children, they need hospitals and medical facilities to be nearby in case of emergencies. All of that would seem to be patently obvious, yet previous attempts to build this kind of international technopolis have failed precisely because their prospective developers failed to recognize this seemingly fundamental need.

Learning from these mistakes, the developers of Songdo got to work immediately constructing residential buildings and other housing, schools, and hospitals—in short, all of the things communities need to grow and thrive, and which contribute to the higher "quality of life" to which people living in those communities aspire. Even before that—in consideration of the need for workers and others to get in and out of Songdo easily and even while that city's residential support infrastructure was still being built—the developers constructed the Incheon Bridge, a 7.4-mile dedicated superbridge that connects Songdo IBD with Incheon International Airport (which has often been ranked as the best modern airport in the world). Incheon Bridge is so magnificent that it has become a tourist attraction in and of itself, and the critical importance of this vital link to the airport earned Songdo immediate attention from many of the world's largest and most successful corporations.

Thus, in shaping the New City, the same priority and emphasis will be placed upon building the people infrastructure first. Moreover, the beauty of the 32-sector Fused Grid design is that we will be able to build out each one in concentric fashion as the need arises. The inclusion of essential services within or near to each neighborhood sector means that they will all be more or less self-sufficient; and as each adjoining segment is added, the quality-of-life infrastructure will only get better as more community amenities are added. Nor will the grid of connector or feeder roads "wall off" the individual neighborhood sectors; rather, they will enable easy and safe travel in and out of those neighborhoods for resident commuters as well as visitors and express-delivery services. In sum, the 32 individual Fused Grid sectors will truly be the building blocks of the New City. And it should be noted that, if we are planning the New City out into the future as far as might be conceivably practical—my target is at least 50 years of viability—we should have contingency plans, if at all possible, for 10% expansion of this modular Fused Grid system.

But here we come to the more radical principle by which I believe the DurantHybrid elevates the Fused Grid into an exciting and innovative urban design for the 21st century. When you look at most contemporary U.S. cities, including

Boston, New York, Dallas, Chicago, and so many others, you see that the tallest buildings tend to be concentrated in the city centers. While there are a few exceptions, usually in places where flat topography allowed unbridled sprawl (Los Angeles comes to mind), approaching these cities by car on the interstate, particularly in the Midwest, can feel like driving toward the Emerald City of Oz—a phalanx of spiky, super-tall skyscrapers all stacked together and towering over a flat-lined horizon. It's almost intimidating; one suddenly realizes how Dorothy must have felt!

Now let's take a 3D look at the New City. We have already established that many of the city's largest structures will be situated around the outer perimeter for a number of very sound reasons ranging from optimizing practical utility of those facilities to ensuring the highest quality of life possible for residents living within the city itself. And as I envision it, much like existing U.S. cities, the New City will contain a suitable and reasonable concentration of beautifully designed high-rise skyscrapers in its center. One might be tempted to refer to center city as the project's "crown jewel," but I am determined to make this entire technopolis a crown jewel!

So, with that in mind, think of the New City as being shaped like a huge sombrero. There is the signature aggregation of gleaming office and municipal government towers in the center, and a ring of major buildings around the outmost perimeter—not as tall as those in center city, but massive in size and scope. But what do we do with the vast expanse of urban real estate extending out in every direction from center to the outer industrial ring? The intuitive, knee-jerk response might be to simply continue with the sloping-sombrero motif, a monotonous pattern in which all of the buildings are gradually shorter and smaller as one moves away from center city.

How boring.

But not only is it boring, such an approach is aesthetically flawed, missing what I believe is a truly wonderful opportunity to enhance the quality of life for every resident, worker, and visitor to the New City. Think about it: What are the essential environmental qualities that virtually every living person—whether country, city, or suburban dweller —values the most when it comes to living, working, and playing spaces in their homes, offices, schools, and parks? I firmly believe that unquestionably, they are light, fresh air, open space, and if possible, a pleasant and unobstructed view of that environment.

This reality is amply demonstrated by the bitterly emotional and viciously combative inner-city battles fought tooth-and-nail between local community residents and often wealthy developers seeking zoning variances to allow the construction of buildings that would drastically exceed existing building-height restrictions, and in effect, isolate local streets while cutting out sunlight and blocking sight lines. Whenever this happens (and it does so quite frequently), local residents are up in arms, cramming into city-council, planning, and zoning-board hearings with their community leaders to acrimoniously fight what they perceive, perhaps quite rightly, as the destruction of their neighborhoods. Unfortunately, most often, they lose. And it is pretty heartbreaking to watch.

So, do you think that light, fresh air, a little extra space, and a decent if limited view out the window is important to a typical city developer? You bet it is!

Therefore, what I envision for the New City is an entirely new and radical approach to the city-wide distribution of buildings—and allocation of building height variations—that will achieve a uniquely spectacular sensory (particularly visual) and aesthetically appealing environment in every city district and locale. The DurantHybrid design makes it possible to strike a critical balance and rhythm among building heights and open views such that in every neighborhood, and from any vantage point anywhere in the city, a resident or visitor will be afforded at least some area of open vista looking out to the horizon, be it from home or office.

The heart of the DurantHybrid model, and what distinguishes it from the standard Fused Grid, is its incorporation of the added dimension of vertical building height to transform the essentially "flat" fused layout into a more multidimensional, or 3D, urban-space design that is user-friendly—and much more importantly, opened up to a much broader platform of building usages and development alternatives. This design will greatly benefit residents, workers, and other users. By utilizing appropriate and reasonable variation of building heights moving from one Fused Grid to the next, as well as from the city center to the outer-network grid modules, we will enable more flexibility and potential diversity in defining the building-usage parameters allowable across the city. This will be so from the city center to the outskirts and back again, and we will tailor those building usages directly to the needs of the people living in each of the 32 Fused Grids. Here's how it works.

Using the time-honored mapping metaphor of the old-fashioned clock face (with apologies to the digital generations!), imagine a line of modern buildings extending from center city and running along the line to one o'clock on the outer ring. Now imagine that the buildings closest to the center, within the innermost ring, are the tallest in the line, perhaps averaging between 60 to 40 stories (or about 700 to 450 feet) tall. As we move along the line to one o'clock, the buildings get progressively shorter, downsizing from about 300 to 120 feet (25 to 10 stories) within the second ring, and finally from about 70 to 30 feet (six to three stories) in the outermost ring. The actual heights and number of stories in this succession of buildings may need to be adjusted to maximize practical utility or other factors; but as a goal, I envision that something approaching a progression of about 45 degrees from the tallest to the shortest building will give the cityscape an optimally pleasing and memorable appearance. I would also stipulate in the urban master plan that a maximum of 80% of all buildings in each ring must comply with zone height requirements. I believe this will allow for some latitude and some creativity with regard to organic building design and development within each zone and ring district.

Now imagine reversing this pattern along the line from center city to three o'clock, with the smallest buildings located in the first ring and the tallest ones placed at the outer part of the third ring and farthest away from center city, at the development's outmost boundary. Next, continue this alternating pattern around the rest of the New City, a line of low-to-high buildings alongside a line of high-to-low ones, as needed. What we have now is a kind of wavy sombrero that evenly distributes a balanced mixture of taller and shorter buildings across all 32 of the Fused Grid neighborhoods, and across the entire city. The immediate virtues and benefits of this widely distributed structural diversity will be that it will accommodate the multipurpose-building usages that I spoke of earlier in this chapter—from residential to office to retail to recreation to open-park green space—either within each of the specific Fused Grid modules, or in immediately adjacent ones. As noted earlier, residents will not have to travel far to get their daily needs or basic essentials (See Figure 9).

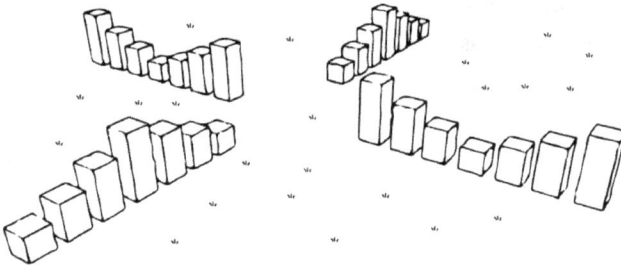

Figure 9: The alternating building height progression of the
DurantHybrid.

But let's look at the DurantHybrid from an urban-
aesthetic perspective. So now imagine that you are standing
somewhere in center city and looking out toward the
perimeter. In one direction, yes, you will be looking at a
wall of other buildings when, in our example, you are
looking toward one o'clock. However, if you simply turn
slightly to your right and look out toward three o'clock,
you will be gazing out at the amazingly open vista that
spans the gracefully rising buildings from the first ring out
to the third ring. And in this scheme a person standing at
any point, anywhere in the city, has the same opportunity:
A 45- to 90-degree turn in any direction will change from a
view of somewhat close-up buildings to an open and
expansive view of the cityscape, culminating with the
countryside beyond and surrounding the horizon itself. The
overall effect of this radically unique configuration will be
both spectacular and breathtaking. One will be afforded all
of the advantages and benefits of city living (including the
remarkable, ubiquitous ambient electronics of this

technopolis), but it will be a city-life experience unlike anything previously experienced anywhere.

Finally, by implementing the full, citywide DurantHybrid Fused Grid design, the development of the New City will accomplish two additional but importantly interrelated things. First, the diversity of building types and ability to handle high user capacity should amply and uniformly provide for the needs of residents and businesses throughout all the neighborhood modules. Ideally (and I deeply desire that this will be the case), such should obviate the need for any of those bitter land-use or zoning-variance legal battles between community residents and developers that have come to be so destructive to the enjoyment of city life and all that it has to offer. Developers will know from the very start what they are permitted to build within each community, business district, and neighborhood. Similarly, local residents will be able to know exactly what they can expect the community to look like, from down the street and around the corner onto the next block to the farthest city limit. In a phrase: There will be room for everybody in the New City.

Hey! Maybe that can be our slogan!

What are the amenities or features about the neighborhood where you live that you most like and enjoy? What negative aspects would you like to change? How can we address neighborhood issues in the New City to make them more livable, safer, and more enjoyable? Post your thoughts on the website at www.BuildTheNewCity.com.

PART III – ACCOMPLISHING THE GOAL: BUILD THE NEW CITY!

Chapter 8 - So How Do We Pay for the New City?

Perhaps you have read all of this "Let's create American jobs!" and "Challenge America to be #1 again!" and "A plan to defeat the rising seas!" stuff and you are thinking: "Well it's all a terrific idea, but how are we going to pay for this great Xanadu or Emerald City that you want us to build? Where is the money going to come from? And *don't dare* tell me it's going to come from my tax dollars!"

Spoken like a true skeptic, taxpayer, and . . . patriot.

You have a right to be skeptical. All too often, and perhaps more than ever over the last several years of the current recession, we have seen colossally wasteful attempts, mostly on the part of government, to shore up our economy merely by throwing money at our problems. We have seen corporate and bank bailouts involving astronomical—nearly incomprehensible—sums of money. The same can be said for the staggering billions of dollars that the U.S. pours into foreign wars or showers on corrupt governments desperately trying to buy their friendship and cooperation—often just to keep them shipping us that damned crude oil. You are right to be skeptical of where the money will come from to build the New City when you read that our national debt just topped $16 TRILLION in September of 2012.

I hope this does not shock you, but I do not have a great deal to say about the ways and means to finance the incredibly massive undertaking to build the New City. I do have some definitive and critically important principles that I strongly believe must be strictly incorporated into the very framework of the financial package that will, and must be put together to make the New City a reality. I will have more to say about that shortly. First, however, let me say this. I know one thing. When there is a buck to be made, American corporations, American financial institutions, and American entrepreneurs, go-getters, business people, and line workers are all right on it. When Americans are convinced that building the New City will create hundreds of thousands of jobs, that it will jumpstart a renewed prosperity for our country, and that it is a truly worthwhile goal for America on the order of our WWII effort and the moon landing—PLUS they can make a few bucks on it—Americans will get it done.

Five Principles

Now to those several principles I mentioned:

First, federal and state governments absolutely must not be involved in any aspect of the funding for the development and building of the New City. Let's face it: Government involvement would only serve to muck everything up; and with the formidable amount of capital that will be required in this venture, the potential for embezzlement, misappropriation of funds, or out-and-out theft will be enough to make any bureaucrat salivate. Clearly, government must be kept out of any participation in the financial orchestration. And to put this in a more positive light, I see a tremendous private investment opportunity in this grand project through which corporations, venture capitalists, and everyday individuals can participate and make money by having a stake in the New City project, whether that is through constructing the buildings and infrastructure, trading in real-estate or business services, or simply buying municipal bonds. When all of these ingredients are right, it is time for government to step aside and let the free-market economy do what it does best: Make money for private and individual interests; build great, prosperous things for the country; and do both of these without overburdening the government or taxpayers with the financial risks.

With that said, there is one interesting new finance model that has been put forth by Henry Cisneros; it does involve government in a limited (and therefore, perhaps manageable) way. In his article "New Funding for New Infrastructure," Cisneros describes this conceptual model as a "public-private partnership in which government obtains funding from private entities, which in turn derive revenue from the projects." However, Cisneros goes on to state, "This is most applicable to high-risk, potentially high-return infrastructure projects such as toll roads and bridges in underdeveloped areas, public-entertainment venues, or even communications systems" (Cisneros, 2012).

In other words, the public-private-partnership funding mechanism that Cisneros describes may be most applicable to the kinds of general-use infrastructure projects that have traditionally fallen under the responsibility of government public works in the past, such as roads, bridges, and communications, as Cisneros mentions, or perhaps mass-transit and other systems that serve the general public interest. However, it remains to be seen if the inclusion of private interests, presumably by corporations and private investors, will serve to make government more accountable by ensuring that the funds are spent wisely and not wasted (and *certainly* not misappropriated). It may well do so, in which case some sort of public-private partnership may indeed be very useful in underwriting the basic, nuts-and-bolts infrastructure requirements of the New City. But I still see private enterprise—and private investment—as the primary vehicle for building the other elements of the city.

Beyond that, the only role that I see for both federal and state government—and in point of fact it is a very valuable one—will be to aggressively remove the kinds of onerous, downright crushing building codes and development restrictions that have made it virtually impossible for any individual or corporation to build something new, good, and financially viable in this country for decades. These are business-killing restrictions that have crushed free enterprise and poisoned entrepreneurship in America to such an extent that it really should be no surprise to anyone why those entrepreneurs and businesspeople have taken their efforts, ideas, and dreams overseas. If our government wants to help, *that* is what they can do to support the New City. And that would be enough from them!

Actually, there are a couple of other things that the government can do to help, but I'll get to those ideas a little later on in this chapter.

So the second principle is really the flipside of the first. The funding of the New City must come entirely from private enterprise and investment. I think that the potential rewards to companies that will build the city and to those who will eventually make it their headquarters are readily apparent. The ultramodern residential, office, and retail space that will be created will be valuable and desirable real estate that will quickly attract buyers and business tenants. Large companies moving their headquarters to the New City will find an abundant supply of educated and skilled people to join their workforces. I truly believe that many young people from the generation that has grown up with the computer and the iPod (and all ensuing generations) will flock to the New City, lured by its technological superiority and its promise of a new, highly exciting, and potentially prosperous—but still challenging —lifestyle in the most advanced urban center ever built.

Finally on this point, once the New City is built, perhaps even before it is completed, there will be a fantastic opportunity for American business and industry to take what is learned from its construction and development and turn that knowledge into a multibillion-dollar export industry. Because as fast as the American population is growing, other populations around the world are growing faster. Foreign countries around the world will be looking for ways to provide decent housing and livelihoods for their people. Furthermore, some of those countries face an even greater threat from rising seas because so much of their populations are concentrated along low-lying coastal areas. Remember that the great tsunami of 2004 killed 230,000 people in 14 countries from India to Indonesia. While that disaster was caused by a massive earthquake, climate change resulting in rising ocean levels simply worsens the potential for an even greater future catastrophe. The people at risk must eventually be relocated.

What greater opportunity for profitable enterprise could there be? As the New City rises in America, a consortium of U.S. companies with American engineers, designers, technicians, and construction line workers takes that knowledge and knowhow overseas to build a hundred new cities around the world. The possibilities, and the potential thereof, would truly seem to be endless.

Building the New City will require huge investment and innovative financial support. We can't fund the New City without your input and ideas. Go to the website www.BuildTheNewCity.com and post your thoughts and suggestions.

Third, there is another division of the U.S. government that I strongly feel must be kept out of the New City project —the military. I have tremendous respect for the men and women of our armed forces, and I support our troops in the dangerous work they must do. This is not a political book, and I do not intend to pass judgment on U.S. policy as it pertains to military action here or abroad. What I am referring to in the context of the construction of the New City is that we have a tendency in America, when it comes to development projects of this magnitude, to call in organizations like the U.S. Army Corps of Engineers (USACE) essentially, to prepare the ground—clear the land, build dams and levees, and do the "grunt work," if you will allow that phrase.

However, as I have stressed all along, I strongly believe that the New City will be best served—and American citizens as a whole will also be best served—by keeping this as much a privately based and funded project as is possible. My vision is of a concerted, free-enterprise-driven effort on the part of corporations and individuals working together to make this happen, with as little use of taxpayer dollars as possible. The only exception, as I mentioned earlier, might be made with respect to the transportation and other infrastructures that will benefit society as a whole.

And yet I do have an idea that I believe will be of tremendous benefit to our military. How is this for a novel idea to support our troops: I have tried to stress throughout this book that one of the noblest, most inspiring aspects of this project is that it is a peacetime crusade rather than one devoted to war and destruction. Instead of building bombs and missiles that are destroyed after they blow up things (and kill people), we will be placing homes and schools and hospitals and skyscrapers—things of lasting value to people. When our political leaders finally come to grips with the fact that we must reduce the size of our military for both economic reasons (a $16 trillion-and-climbing national debt) and practical ones (the need to change our defense strategies from massive land, sea, and air battles to fighting pinpointed terrorism and cyberwar), what do you say we offer jobs in the New City to all of our U.S. servicemen and women after they are honorably discharged from duty? Chances are that many of our military men and women will already have the proper training and career skills sorely needed at every level of expertise to build a brand-new city from the ground up. If some of them don't, we can train them at the technical schools and training centers that will be an integral part of the educational system provided in the New City (see the Education section of Chapter 6).

We'll turn soldiers into steelworkers, and pilots into computer programmers. Through a program of intensive education and apprenticeship, we'll train former military personnel (and other people, of course) specifically targeting the jobs for which there is the most need at any given time. Need construction workers? Electricians? Technicians? The training centers will adjust accordingly and provide trained specialists suited to every job. Not only that, but we can both reward and thank our military men and women by making them eligible for low-cost or even free training in the trade, professional, or technological/scientific fields of their choice. In a way, this would be the modern equivalent of the post–World War II GI Bill that enabled thousands of soldiers returning from battle to go to college and thus have a bright future in civilian life.

This could very conceivably be a win-win for everybody involved including, ironically, the politicians. How? Instead of facing the excruciatingly painful task of closing military bases and showing our dedicated soldiers the door with no options and little hope of establishing a new civilian life, politicians will be able to say, "We have provided for you. Here is a broad menu of opportunities for immediate employment and permanent relocation in superior housing in communities with great schools for your kids." (Even though the politicians will have had nothing to do with it! Well, we'll let them have their fun.)

But seriously, the bottom line is that we can put people to work instead of putting them in harm's way in foreign wars that simply do not seem to be serving our national interests any longer. Let me say once more—I promise for the last time—that this is not a political book, and I do not wish to dabble in the foreign-policy decisions of the United States. However, I will go this far: I will say without reservation that I firmly believe that the export opportunities that will grow out of the "Build a New City" movement here in the U.S., those generated by the building of new, technologically advanced cities in countries all around the world and vastly improving the quality of life of their people, will go immensely further toward winning the hearts and minds of our adversaries and those that fear us than war and bombs and destruction ever will.

The fourth recommendation that I wish to make is that we must issue millions of dollars in municipal bonds that will serve to raise money for the building of the city. The bonds must be made available in all denominations, large and small, and to all Americans so that everybody can participate and have a stake in investing and earning dividends built upon the successful development of the city. Don't get me wrong; I certainly encourage large corporate and banking investors as well. The big-boy investors will be essential to our success; and certainly, 401k, hedge-fund and retirement-management firms will want a piece of the action (which in turn will benefit American workers who are members of those plans). All I am saying here is that the big investors must not be permitted to gobble up all or most of the municipal bonds. We must ensure that the average man or woman on the street can participate—they must not be shut out. Remember what I said earlier: This is a project by Americans for Americans. What better way to unite the country behind a great cause than to invite every American to have a piece of the pie?

Alongside unknotting the bureaucratic logjam of petty regulations and restrictions on free enterprise and development, the issuance of bonds is yet another way that our federal government can provide immeasurable help in making the New City both a gleaming reality and a real source of American pride in accomplishment. Because in order to encourage every American to buy those municipal bonds, they must of course be federally underwritten by the Federal Deposit Insurance Corporation (FDIC) or some other agency. If the FDIC is not presently authorized to insure this type of municipal-bond instrument, then I firmly believe that our political leaders must immediately get to work on writing the appropriate legislation toward creating a new agency that will be so empowered and authorized.

This last principle may ultimately be the most important one. I believe that the workers who build the New City must be paid well. We heard a great deal during the critical 2012 presidential election year about the haves and the have-nots, about the one-percenters versus the 99-percenters, and about the conflict between wealth distribution and access to wealth and prosperity in this country. And all of this is another political maelstrom that I do not go into in this book.

What I do believe, however, is that people who work a full-time job of 35 to 40 or more hours a week ought to be able to earn enough money to afford a home, however modest, and to raise their families while saving at least some money for their children's education, their own retirement, and perhaps a little bit to spend on a decent vacation once in a while. There are far too many jobs in our country, such as in retail or restaurant and food service, where the average salaries are so low that disposable income is simply not available, and people are forced to work two or three jobs to make up the difference. People who work in the New City ought to be able to live there— not necessarily in its ritzier, more well-to-do neighborhoods —but there ought to be districts where they can afford to reside in reasonable comfort while not constantly worrying about paying the bills. That I why I have called for a reasonable range of affordable housing to be built into as many of the Fused Grid modules as possible (see Chapter 7), so that most of the employed residents of the city will be able to live relatively near to where they work. I believe that ensuring a mixed-usage plan for each of the Fused Grid modules will encourage a range of income among inhabitants, and foster ethnic and cultural diversity among the residents that live in each sector, thereby enhancing the diversity of the city as a whole.

How do we accomplish this? How do we structure the employment rules for an entire city to make sure that we are paying decent, livable wages to the people building the city, from the engineers and managers right down to the construction laborers?

One radical idea of mine is to tie each company CEO's salary to that of the laborers—if the CEO wants another $1 million in salary, the workers get another $10 per hour in base pay. But okay, I guess I have to concede that this would never fly. No CEO in the world would ever agree to such a thing! But the contracts that the major developers of the New City project will sign must contain some sort of living-wage requirement. And let me be clear about what I mean by a "living wage." I am talking about hourly wages or salaries that are much higher than what is stipulated by today's "minimum wage" laws, which—let's be perfectly honest—are tragically too low, and which are impossible for anyone to support a family on, much less afford a decent home or send their kids to college. The minimum wage is one reason why so many people are forced to work two or more jobs just to make ends meet. The living wages that are paid to workers by the developers of the New City and the corporations that locate there must involve hourly rates (or annual salaries) that are considerably more acceptable than the so-called minimum wage. If that means that the people living in the city will ultimately pay a bit more for goods and services, so be it, because I also strongly believe that the living wage will elevate the general standard of living throughout the city, benefiting everyone through prosperous commerce and vigorous business activity. In sum, people should have some money in their pockets!

I submit that the companies themselves can do a number of things to help ensure that all workers are well paid. Let me back up a little bit by pointing out that companies will have a ready supply of qualified workers thanks to the educational training centers that will be set up throughout the city (see the Education section in Chapter 6). Therefore, employers should expect to provide better-than-average pay for new employees, who will be able to step in and contribute to profitability immediately. In addition, perhaps during the early construction phases, these companies might provide free or subsidized housing for laborers and their families, at least for the term of each building phase. These subsidized apartments or homes would represent significant federal- and state-tax write-offs for the construction companies, and while I am not in principle a big fan of giving massive tax breaks to huge corporations, in this case the write-offs would directly benefit the workers—perhaps more than they would the companies.

Corporations could also offer profit-sharing plans, or even modest stock-option plans, to all workers on their payroll without exception. Just think of the incentive that such plans would give to workers to do the best job possible in order to make the New City such a success that they see the results in their profit-sharing accounts, or in the progressively rising value of the company stock they would own (which itself is accruing more shares as they labor in their higher paying jobs). The ironic thing about some of these ideas is that they are really a throwback to the great building booms in America's history, when everyone had a stake in the success of the project, and everyone thus wanted it to succeed for the benefit of all rather than simply a wealthy few.

There are at least two other constructive things that the federal government can do to help ensure that workers are paid as well as possible. First, they can reduce payroll taxes on the construction and other companies involved in building and outfitting the New City—with the provision that at least part of that money be used to augment the salaries of the line workers and laborers. Our political and business leaders might need to take a thorough look at other sorts of "invisible" taxes and fees that are presently paid to the government, and place a burden on those companies when it comes to hiring and fairly compensating their workforces.

Second, particularly with respect to those hopefully limited projects that will most likely require government involvement—such as the infrastructure of roads, bridges, rail, and utilities—the government can offer incentives to the contracting companies such as bonus payments for early completion of various construction phases. Furthermore, I would include a firm stipulation in those contracts that a fair percentage of such bonus payments—I believe that a 50/50 split between workers and companies would be most appropriate—must be shared among all of the worker-employees of the companies that qualify by completing projects ahead of schedule. Here again, this will serve the dual purpose of creating a tangible incentive for the line workers to do the very best, most efficient job possible for their company, while at the same time creating an opportunity to increase the incomes of all of the workers as something that is worked for and earned for the benefit of everyone involved. Better income for the builders and eventual residents of the New City will translate into prosperity, a higher standard of living, and a better quality of life overall.

Let's see what we can do to provide a living wage to all workers!

A Peacetime Challenge Instead of War

I want to close this chapter by acknowledging that the New City will be a very expensive project. Furthermore, the likelihood is that some pessimistic naysayers may be inclined to overlook all the great benefits that will come from building the New City, focusing only on the cost. They will ignore any cost/benefit analysis, even more so any social benefits, throw up their hands, and narrow-mindedly say, "It will cost too much."

To the skeptics—and indeed, to everyone else who reads this book—let me say this: I'll tell you what has cost too much. Our wars in Iraq and Afghanistan, with incursions into Pakistan, have been staggeringly expensive—in dollars spent, and more critically, in lives lost. A recent study from Brown University estimates the total cost of these wars at between *$3.2 to $4 trillion*, not to mention the over 6,000 American lives and as many as 236,000 lives overall lost.

I have stressed throughout this book that the New City is a peacetime project that will benefit our country for decades to come. It will put people to work at a time when unemployment is over eight percent—right where it was during the height of the Great Depression. It will be an economic engine that will drive our country forward; and perhaps most importantly, it will be an inspiration to all

Americans, something in which can truly take pride. It is difficult to assess precisely how much it will cost to build the New City, but how about this for starters? What if we took $4 trillion and spent in on something *for* the United States *in* the United States? What if we spent it on a project that will have lasting value, rather than on bombs and missiles that only reap destruction and are themselves destroyed when they are used? Or on tanks and fighter jets that have only one purpose, that of war—and are otherwise are of no practical use whatsoever. Once you realize how much military equipment the United States discards in the desert amid troop evacuation after one of our wars (because it's too expensive to bring it all home), you will be shocked and outraged at the sheer waste of it all. And of course, there is the matter of 6,000 American heroes whose lives can never be brought back.

What if we took that $4 trillion and instead spent it on America, on an investment that will enhance lives instead of taking them? Wouldn't that be a worthwhile down payment on a project to build the greatest city the world has ever seen?

I think so. What do you think? Post your opinion on the website at www.BuildTheNewCity.com.

Chapter 9 – Restoring Coastal Areas and Tidal Wetlands

As we proceed with the building of the New City, and as we populate it over time, we will be relocating thousands of people from those coastal areas of our country that are at serious risk from the global phenomenon of the rising sea levels, which, if the present trend continues, will eventually —and inevitably—be inundated and overtaken by those rising seas. Some of these low-lying areas will become uninhabitable—they will essentially morph with the ocean ecosystem; and parts of some cities, as well as many small towns, are likely to be lost forever. The configuration of the coastline in these regions will be altered. Presumably, the shoreline will move inward until reaching equilibrium with higher ground, and a new shoreline will be established.

What are we to do about these coastal regions? Shall we simply abandon them to the ocean and allow the once-thriving shore towns to become the underwater equivalent of Dust Bowl Western ghost towns? I have a better idea. Because I believe that despite the fact that the rising of the seas might appear to be nothing more or less than a complete and utter natural disaster, there is a silver lining— a golden opportunity—to this apparent catastrophe that we can (and *must*) exploit. Let's consider a somewhat simple future scenario in these areas as the sea level rises.

First, as mentioned earlier, over time the lowest-lying regions and the towns within them will simply be inundated and disappear altogether. I say "over time" because I want to be clear that this will be a long process—it certainly will not happen overnight like a tsunami. However, as was discussed in Chapter 2, the worst-case scientific scenarios appear to predict a gradual rise in ocean levels of two to four inches over the next decade or two—certainly not insignificant by any means, but granting us a modicum of time to act.

I also want to point out that ecologically valuable areas such as tidal marshes or wetlands will also disappear. As a stark example, if the IPCC's 2007 projections for sea-level increases prove true, an astounding 50% of Florida's Everglades National Park will disappear, according to Larry Perez, the park's Science Liaison Communications Officer (www.atlanticrising.org/case-studies/view.asp?id=40). But as the ocean pushes inland, it will naturally transform some of those inland areas into new marshland. In essence, the shoreline will change but the tidal ecosystem will, in all likelihood, simply be substantially relocated—that is, moved farther inland.

But despite all of this seemingly bad news, there is a tremendous opportunity here, both for a measured and well-planned reclamation of ecologically important wetlands (or the creation of new ones), and for American job seekers. The National Oceanographic and Aeronautics Administration (NOAA) estimates that environmental-habitat restoration projects, such as dam removal to restore free-flowing rivers, or the restoration of coastal wetlands that we are talking about here, typically create about 17 jobs per every $1 million invested—and in some cases as many as 33 jobs per $1 million! (www.nmfs.noaa.gov/ stories/012/09/09_04_2012_habitat_restoration_video.

html) Compare that with the number of jobs created with every $1 million invested in the oil-and-gas sector (5 jobs) and road-and-highway infrastructure (7 jobs), and you can easily see the terrific opportunity that we will have for putting thousands of additional people to work in habitat restoration and reclamation. Furthermore, NOAA points out that habitat restoration creates a wider variety of jobs than either infrastructure improvement or the oil or gas industries; construction workers, landscapers, heavy-equipment operators, and technical experts such as engineers and wildlife biologists are all gainfully employed and doing important work. Much of this cleanup will simply be erasing man's footprint on the land—the kind of roll-up-your-sleeves-and-get-dirty work that could employ thousands of laborers. Finally, according to NOAA, restoration projects create demand for local industries, such as plant nurseries and quarries; and, of course, habitat-restoration jobs can't be outsourced to foreign countries!

Another important consideration is that asking people to relocate is a very difficult thing to do, particularly in the case of those for whom life in the New City, for all of its conveniences and amenities, will still be radically and perhaps unnervingly different from the one they knew in their tight-knit coastal communities and towns. Many will resist relocation despite the New City's perks and advantages; some will refuse to leave despite the risk of staying in the coastal danger zones. We can logically expect that the people most likely to refuse to leave will be the ones that made their livelihoods from the local land and the sea—the fishermen, crabbers, clammers, and shrimpers, or the charter-boat owners catering to the tourist trade—people whose families, like so many along the Gulf from Texas to Florida, have lived and thrived there for five or six generations or more. It is thus quite reasonable to expect that such folks will not want to leave, and many will not have to.

To begin with, we will put people to work in both habitat restoration and the removal of manmade buildings and infrastructural developments endangered by the advancing oceanfront. Some buildings may be worth relocating farther inland; others will need dismantling. Some of the original construction materials may be salvageable or recyclable. Some cemeteries may need relocation. With regard to the natural habitat, some local dams and manmade landscape features may need to be destroyed or removed to allow the ecosystem time to organically reestablish itself. I think that it is our responsibility to do this work for the sake of our environment; we should remove the scars of man's presence in these areas, to whatever extent that this is practical, so that they will once again be naturally beautiful. However, as the NOAA report makes clear, there are also sound economic reasons for doing so.

We must see the opportunity that lies in the apparent adversity of this impending phenomenon. As I've said throughout this book, whatever the cause, rising seas are a scientific fact, and we must develop a productive and proactive response. As I see it, this is a unique opportunity to harness the forces of nature and restore the coastal areas that will be deeply affected. We can correct some of the wrongs that we have done, such as building too close to beaches and tidal lowlands in the first place, and then overpopulating those areas to the point that pollution and habitat destruction became major problems for both the human beings and wildlife living there. And in the long run we can see to it that the "new" coastline is a recreational paradise for vacationers, be they beachgoers, boaters and fishermen, or nature lovers wanting to experience the flora and fauna. We can create, or re-create as the case may be, a thriving waterfront string of towns and communities filled with businesses and services devoted to serving the tourist and recreation crowd.

There are places in our country where habitat reclamation consists of little more than trucking millions of tons of sand and dumping it onto ever-eroding beaches in a never-ending effort to save them. This "solution," if one can call it that, is often politically controversial because beach restoration benefits the well-to-do landowners of waterfront property, and to a lesser extent beachfront towns and communities, but it is almost always paid for from taxpayer dollars. But with the reclamation effort that I envision—an aggressively proactive plan to deal head-on with the potential crisis of rising seas—we have a genuine opportunity to do coastal-habitat restoration right.

Whether you live in an urban region or a rural one, if natural habitate reclamation is important to you, post your thoughts—or criticisms—on the website at www.BuildTheNewCity.com.

Chapter 10 – Conclusion: Let's Build The New City!

We live in the greatest country in the world, but I believe we must acknowledge that we have some serious problems to face both now and as we plunge ahead into the 21st Century. As I said in the very beginning of this book, Americans today seem to be more deeply divided than ever before in our history. At the same time, we have never been more stubborn in embracing polarized viewpoints and simply refusing to compromise or even engage in productive dialogue. This dichotomy is amply, and perhaps distressingly evidenced by our closely fought Presidential elections, in which we seem to be evenly split over the candidates, the major parties, and the positions for which they appear to stand. Many would argue that the 2000 presidential election was decided in Florida's Supreme Court rather than by the ballot box, and the polarity of the electorate seems only to have gotten worse and more vitriolic in the 12 years since. In Congress, the American notion of compromise appears to have been all but abandoned. Our congressional leaders dig in their heels out of so-called "principle" on everything from economic policy to taxes to election reform to healthcare to energy policy and beyond. Neither side will budge, and as a result nothing seems to get done.

Life is full of challenges, but what is different today is that our leadership seems unwilling to fix or even acknowledge some of the most obvious, basic problems facing our nation. What are these problems? Here's a complete review in which it is important—and I think really exciting—to note how the New City project addresses every concern, as I will summarize later in this chapter:

◆Education: It widely acknowledged and accepted that education is the single most important aspect of a free and open society and nation. Education is indeed our most important investment in children and their future. Of the top 20 global economies, only in the U.S. do large segments of our leadership want to cut education funding. Meanwhile, our children lag behind those of other nations in educational proficiency.

◆Healthcare: The U.S. is the only modern economy that does not provide basic healthcare. A large number of our Congressional leaders want to retreat from whatever progress we have made with health-care reform by completely scrapping the Patient Protection and Affordable Care Act of 2010—a case, in my view, of throwing out the baby with the bathwater, rather than just offering more productive suggestions or recommendations how we can make it better of fix some of its flaws. This is hardly a sign of competent, thoughtful, or resourceful leadership.

◆Defense spending: The U.S. spends more on the military and defense than the next 14 nations *combined*, and that of course includes both China and Russia, whose aggregate total is less than one third of what America spends. And making that figure even more absurd, we are allies with virtually all of those countries except China and Russia. So the question is: Why are we spending so much? Why can we not come to grips with the need to reduce our military—while keeping it strong and adapted to fighting the new threats of terrorism and localized hostilities from rogue nations or despots? Our leadership on both sides of the political aisle simply refuses to touch this issue, particularly when it comes to closing military bases in their respective voting districts that have become unnecessary or obsolete. Of course, the surface concern here is votes, although the underlying issue is providing otherwise-scarce jobs to people as the economy continues to languish, which brings me to my next point.

✦Employment: In bad times especially, we tend to look to government to do something to "create jobs." In an election year, we hear over and over again how both parties claim they will create jobs to spur the economy. In my view, it is not discussed often enough whether government can really create jobs, or whether its true role should be to establish the business-friendly environment in which job growth will flourish, as many economists believe. The answer does not lie in passing a few infrastructure-redevelopment bills, which might get approved in Congress . . . or never voted on, or filibustered. The answer also does not lie in making the government the employer of last resort, thus only expanding our government and adding millions to our tax burden. In short, there have been no sound plans or strategies on the part of government to create or foster job growth within the economy. There is rancor, accusation, and name-calling between political parties, and certainly no substantive or creative solutions are being proposed.

✦Climate Change: Every other nation on Earth accepts the scientific facts about climate change and the need to work cooperatively to mitigate its effects and prevent its acceleration. America stands embarrassingly alone and debates the reality that is right before our eyes.

Fixing the Worst Problem of All

Finally, the most insidious and disturbing problem that I see facing America is a pervasive sense of pessimism and hopelessness about the prospects of significantly improving our situation. We seem to have simply lost our spirit and our drive to achieve something better for ourselves and our country. We seem resigned to mediocrity, and I find that pathetic.

We see that our government is not working, and many of our institutions seem to have likewise failed us. In our Congress, political ideology trumps reasonable compromise, and when that happens government no longer governs—by which I mean running the country and doing the will of the people who voted them in, and doing so for the benefit of all, not just the wealthy and well-connected few. Our political leaders in both parties retreat to their ideological corners, both sides proclaiming themselves to be the "true" defenders of the Constitution. Worse yet, our Congressional leaders are primarily beholden to the special-interest groups that spend millions, possibly billions, on getting them elected—wealthy individuals, organizations, and corporations that most often are not even a part of the voter constituency of the politicians they have bought and sold.

With regard to American corporations, despite flirting with bankruptcy and being saved by government bailouts via billions of taxpayer dollars, corporate profits continue to soar to record highs. Calls for banking reform seem to have achieved nothing, and CEOs and other company leaders continue to enjoy obscene salary packages, perks, stock options, and golden parachutes. They are still rewarded for driving up share values, even if that means eliminating basic jobs and laying off thousands of everyday people. In this climate, corporations sit on billions of dollars in profits, refusing to create jobs themselves, and blaming their inaction on the uncertainty of Washington's direction and leadership——a vicious circle of inaction and ineptitude.

For all the talk of job creation and of business and political uncertainty in this election year, corporate profits have undeniably reached record levels, while worker incomes have been flat—or even receded, in some cases. And it seems that corporations always get bailed out— while ordinary folks face foreclosure and are forced to file for bankruptcy.

In my upbringing, I was taught that it is not acceptable to simply complain about one's problems; you only get to sound off if you can also offer a valid, workable solution or positive direction for change. Well, in this book, I am complaining, and I believe that things in our country do not have to be this way—and *I have a solution* that will address all of these problems to some degree, but that most particularly offers tangible resolutions for three of the most vexing issues we now face: Jobs, climate-change preparedness, and the hopelessness that hangs over America like a raincloud. I propose that Americans stop waiting for our government to act—it is doubtful that they ever will as they stand up in Congress on the political stump and spout venomous oratory against the other party —indeed anyone who disagrees with their positions. I have trumpeted the phrase that the New City is a project "For America, by Americans," and I propose that building it is essentially a people's crusade, and our government must either facilitate this venture or just get out of the way.

Let's briefly recap how building the New City will provide valuable solutions to the problems outlined earlier in this chapter, and by doing so, will breathe new life and inspiration into our American spirit. And I encourage you to add your own thoughts by visiting the website at www.BuildTheNewCity.com.

Education: Ambient intelligence (AmI) that is built into the very infrastructure of the New City will make quality schooling available to every student equally and affordably. Computerized intelligent linkups within homes and schools will ensure access to lesson instruction for students; enable teachers to monitor the progress of each and every student, and further, this technology and access will enable those students in need of remedial assistance to get it at any time of the day or night, and anywhere as well. In the New City, the expression "No child left behind" will be an educational reality rather than a hollow political platitude.

Healthcare: While the issue of spiraling healthcare cost may still require some creative thought in order to optimize it, access to health care in the New City will not. Here again, AmI will enable close and effective monitoring of those who may be at risk for health issues, or who may have chronic physical concerns. AmI will give doctors immediate access to patient records to offer instantaneous lifesaving diagnoses and treatment. This alone may help to cut costs by providing "pinpoint" necessary treatments or hospitalizations and eliminating unnecessary ones. And individual privacy will be respected; people who do not wish to be monitored in this manner may simply opt out of the programs.

Defense Spending: I have pointed out that the one aspect of reducing our military that strikes fear in the hearts of politicians everywhere in America is the prospect of losing obsolete and over-manned military bases (make that "votes") within their constituent districts. The New City provides what I believe is a reasonable and even attractive alternative to simply putting our dedicated military men and women back onto the civilian streets with no appreciable options or employment prospects. I don't even care if our congressmen and congresswomen "take credit" for the New City's policy of providing homes, technical training and livelihoods for honorably discharged military folks. (We'll all know the real truth!) And just as importantly, we can take some of our outrageously bloated defense spending and perhaps use some of that money toward the construction and development of the New City infrastructure of roads, bridges, and communications systems.

Employment: On the practical side, I do not think that anyone will argue the point that the most urgent and deeply felt need in America right now is jobs, jobs, jobs. We don't just need thousands of jobs, or even hundreds of thousands of jobs—we need millions of jobs. Because a great many good things happen to a society and a culture and across whole communities simply by putting people to work. Steady and reliable employment, of course, puts money in people's pockets that they will start to spend, which will in turn drive the economy forward and productivity upward. But it does much more than that. It dramatically changes attitudes, and fosters hopefulness and optimism for the future. It encourages people to strive and to plan for the betterment of their lives and those of their families instead of hunkering down waiting for the hammer to fall. As we saw in Table 1 in Chapter 1, which is re-presented below as Table 3, building the New City will generate as many as 276,000 jobs through industries supporting the construction effort, as well as through concurrent habitat restoration and the evacuation of waterfront regions in the coastal areas on the verge of yet another deadly disaster caused by rising oceans. Now think about the possibilities if we decided to build *two* New Cities!

TABLE 3. POTENTIAL JOB CREATION IN BUILDING
THE NEW CITY

PROJECT TYPE	ESTIMATED NUMBER OF JOBS
City Construction	100,000–150,000
Airport	10,000–12,000
Rail Station	8,000–10,000
Nuclear-Power Plant	3,500–4,500
Water-Delivery Plant	3,000–4,000
Wastewater-Treatment Facility	3,000–4, 000
Trucking/Delivery of Materials	1,000–1,500
NATIONWIDE	
Manufacturing (Building materials)	40,000–50,000
Technical/Engineering/ Architectural	5,000–10,000
Environmental-Habitat Restoration	20,000–30,000
Total Estimated Job Generation	193,500–276,000

Climate Change: America, both our government and our people, must take off the blinders and accept the scientifically proven reality that the Earth's icecaps are melting at an alarming—and accelerating—rate; and that as a direct consequence, sea levels around the world are rising dangerously. I have stressed throughout this book that I have no intention of getting caught up in the seriously over-politicized firestorm of debate as to whether this phenomenon is strictly a natural one or whether man is in part or even wholly responsible. Because it IS happening, no matter what you choose to believe about man's involvement, and we must pull together and do something about it by proactively carrying out a solid and workable plan to move people out of those coastline areas facing imminent destruction, and do so before it is too late. The New City provides at least a beginning phase of this highly humanitarian mission that I believe we owe to our own people.

Building the New City elegantly solves three major challenges at once. First, the country MUST create jobs—not just hundreds of thousands of jobs but millions of them. Second, the country MUST prepare and provide for population growth and the inevitable rising of the seas and their subsequent impact on coastal communities. Finally, when was the last time we had national pride? When was the last time we all worked together to overcome a colossal challenge to our way of life, or to achieve something truly great for our nation and our people? When was the last time we were inspired to reach for an achievement that stands as one of the greatest accomplishments in the annals of human history because, in the words of President Kennedy, "that challenge is one that we are willing to accept, one we are unwilling to postpone, and one which we intend to win"?

Building the New City will be this nation's first great, inspirational challenge of the 21st century. It is a project strictly by Americans for Americans that all Americans can share in one form or another and be fiercely proud of. And as America always does, it represents a greater good that America will ultimately share with the entire world.

Let's build the New City!

Todd Durant

Epilogue and Challenge to America: This Book Is Intended to Create Thought!

This is an ideas book. Critics may review my proposals and charge that this book is long on theory and short on substance. My response, which I give you here in advance, is that I am not a master urban planner, and I do not have all of the answers to the problems afflicting our economy; the woes of our cities in the face of impending planetary climate change; or the issues regarding our cultural, social, and political resolve as a free nation. Obviously these are hugely complicated and important issues.

When President John F. Kennedy boldly declared in 1961 that we would put a man on the moon, neither he nor any of the brilliant scientists at NASA (or anywhere else) had any idea of how we were going to do that. It was a magnificent challenge to America. Kennedy was willing to back that promise with tremendous financial support of up to $531 million in fiscal 1962 and between $7 and $9 billion over the following five years. But consider what he said later in a speech given at Rice University in September 1962:

"We choose to go to the moon in this decade and do the other things, not because they are easy, but because they are hard, *because that goal will serve to organize and measure the best of our energies and skills,* because that challenge is one that we are willing to accept, one we are unwilling to postpone, and one which we intend to win, and the others, too" [*emphasis mine*].

Similarly, in 1939 Albert Einstein sent a letter to President Franklin Roosevelt (which was actually written by his physicist colleague Leo Szilard) in which he rather cautiously (but urgently) warned the President about the possibility of the creation of the atomic bomb. He said that, "[I]t may be possible to set up a nuclear chain reaction in a large mass of uranium, by which vast amounts of power... would be generated.... This new phenomenon would also lead to the construction of bombs, and it is conceivable—though much less certain—that extremely powerful bombs of a new type may thus be constructed." (Cited from Bronowski,1973.)

Einstein was always conservative and humble in his public pronouncements (if not those to the scientific community, it was certainly true of his dealings with the non-scientific community). Thus, in the letter to Roosevelt, Einstein probably said less than he knew, or believed he knew. But even he was not sure about how nuclear power might be harnessed—for good or bad, as evidenced by his statement that the actual means of constructing the bomb was "much less certain."

The point of these two examples is that like the space program and the Manhattan Project, the devil will be in the details as America builds the New City. I believe America needs a worthy peacetime goal upon which we can set our sights and go after with all of the resolve and determination of defeating a wartime threat—but without any of the bloodshed and heartbreak of combat. In any human endeavor as auspicious as the space program or the New

City, mistakes will be made and corrected; innovations developed; and valuable knowledge learned along the way

Not long ago, PBS aired an episode of their long-running series *Nova* entitled "Super Bridge," about the building of the Clark Bridge, a new four-lane suspension bridge on U.S. Route 67 over the Mississippi River at Alton, Illinois. The architects on the project had come up with a radical new design in which the suspension cables supporting the bridge deck would be slung from two monolithic columns located in the middle of the highway between the east- and westbound lanes (rather than the more traditional method of two double-column towers like those of the George Washington or Golden Gate bridges, where the towers extend to the outer edges of the bridge deck). Thus, for the Clark Bridge, the suspension cables would run diagonally from the central towers across the four east-west lanes of the highway (two on either side) to the outer edge of the bridge deck. The successful result is an exquisitely simple and elegant, minimalist design that is breathtakingly simply beautiful to look at.

But what most struck me about its construction, as amply portrayed in the documentary film, was the number of unanticipated problems that the builders encountered "in the field" that had to be addressed and resolved in order to successfully complete construction of the bridge. When we admire magnificent structures that modern man has constructed, from skyscrapers to bridges and dams, we tend to think that everything was precisely planned out at the blueprint stage, that everything that went into building those structures was predesigned to work perfectly, and that every nut and bolt went together like clockwork. But the truth of the matter is this almost never the case. Instead, design modifications and structural or operational adjustments are made continuously on the jobsite.

For example, the engineering design for the Clark Bridge called for the steel suspension cables, each of which was thickly wrapped with a yellow plastic waterproof coating, to be bundled together and drawn through two huge, curved steel pipes or pylons that would sit on the top of each support tower. However, when workers tried to draw the cables through the pipes, excessive amounts of the plastic waterproofing material was scraped off the support cables. Left as is, the exposed cables would quickly rust and weaken, compromising the integrity of the entire structure, and thus the safety of the people crossing the bridge. Numerous alternate procedures for getting the cables through the pipes were attempted, and thankfully a solution was finally found, but this was only one of a dozen or more glitches that were successfully overcome in the course of completing the bridge.

I fully expect that the designers, engineers, and builders of the New City will encounter the same sort of challenges and obstacles that were encountered at Alton—times 1,000! And there is no doubt in my mind whatsoever that we will meet those challenges and overcome those obstacles in innovative ways that will both surprise and inspire us to do even greater things. We will invent new technologies and groundbreaking, ultra-efficient ways of doing things—perhaps a whole new "science" of urban planning and development will be born.

From there, once the New City is built, and America has shown the rest of the world how it is done, I foresee a whole new multi-industrial "cottage industry" for large consortiums of American companies constructing much-needed New Cities all across the world. Thus the New City concept will continue to be a source of good, well-paying jobs for Americans at the financing, development, and engineering levels, even if a large percentage of the laborers—who should also be well compensated—are in fact citizens of the foreign countries. The possibilities, as they say, are endless.

Come with me, then. Let's put our heads together and come up with the stellar ideas and synergies that will make the New City a magnificent, world-renowned feat of engineering achievement and a new symbol of American inspiration and greatness.

What are your ideas? Post them on the website at www.BuildTheNewCity.com.

References

Abowd, G.D., & Mynatt, E.D. (2004). Designing for the human experience in smart environments. In D.J. Cook & S.K. Das (Eds.), *Smart Environments: Technology, Protocols, and Applications* (pp. 153–174). Hoboken, NJ: Wiley.

Augusto, J.C., & McCullagh, P. (2007). Ambient intelligence: Concepts and applications, *Computer Science and Information Systems, 4*(1) 1–28.

Bobick, A.F., Intille, S.S., Davis, J.W., Baird, F., Pinhanez, C.S., Campbell, L.W. et al. (1999). The KidsRoom: A perceptually based interactive and immersive story environment. *Presence 8*(4) 369–393.

Bronowski, J. (1973). *The Ascent of Man.* Boston: Little, Brown.

Cappelli, P. (2012). *Why Good People Can't Get Jobs: The skills gap and what companies can do about it.* Philadelphia: Wharton Digital Press.

Cisneros, H. (January–February 2012). New Funding for New Infrastructure. *cities&towns online,* Downloaded on July 28, 2012, from http://bettercities.net/article/new-funding-new-infrastructure-15872.

Cook, D.J., Augusto, J.C., & Jakkula, V.R. (2007). *Ambient Intelligence: Technologies, Applications, and Opportunities,* Downloaded August 22, 2012 from: http://www.eecs.wsu.edu/~cook/pubs/pmc10.pdf.

Cooper, M. (March 22, 2011). "Nuclear Power Loses Support in New Poll." *The New York Times*.

Das, S.K., Cook, D.J., Bhattacharya, A., Heierman, E.O. III, & Lin, T.-Y. (2002) The Role of Prediction Algorithms in the MavHome Smart Home Architecture. *IEEE Wireless Communications Special Issue on Smart Homes*, (9)6, 77–84.

Engineering News Record. (December, 2011). Korean Creations. New York: McGraw-Hill.

Fischer, G.J. (1949). *A Statistical Summary of Shipbuilding under the U.S. Maritime Commission during World War II*. Washington, D.C.: Historical Reports of War Administration; United States Maritime Commission, no. 2.

Milward, A.S. (1979). *War, Economy, and Society, 1939-1945*. Berkeley: University of California Press.

Pollack, M.E. (2005). Intelligent Technology for an Aging Population: The use of AI to assist elders with cognitive impairment. *AI Magazine, 26*(2) 9–24.

Rao, S. & Cook, D.J. (2003). Identifying Tasks and Predicting Actions in Smart Homes using Unlabeled Data. *Proceedings of the Machine Learning Workshop on the Continuum from Labeled to Unlabeled Data, 2003*.

Sallenger, Jr., A.H., Doran, K.S., & Howd, P.A. (2012). Hotspot of Accelerated Sea-level Rise on the Atlantic Coast of North America. *Nature Climate Change*, published online June 24, 2012.

Shakun, J.D., Clark, P.U., Feng, H., Marcott, S.A., Mix, A.C., Zhengyu, L., Otto-Bliesner, B., Schmittner, A., & Bard, E. (April 2012). Global warming preceded by increasing carbon dioxide concentrations during the last deglaciation (pp. 49–54). *Nature*, 484.

Sivak, M., & Schoettle, B. (2012a). Update: Percentage of young persons with a driver's license continues to drop. *Traffic Injury Prevention*, 13, 341.

Sivak, M., & Schoettle, B. (2012b). Recent changes in the age composition of drivers in 15 countries. *Traffic Injury Prevention*, 13, 126–132.

Strauss, B.H., Ziemlinski, R., Weiss, J.L., & Overpeck, J.T. (2012). Tidally adjusted estimates of topographic vulnerability to sea level rise and flooding in the contiguous United States. Environmental Research Letters, 7; IOP Publishing.

Tassava, C.J. (2005/2008). The American Economy during World War II. EH.Net Encyclopedia, edited by R. Waples, February 10, 2008, URL http://eh.net/encyclopedia/article/tassava.WWII

Tebaldi, C., Strauss, B.H., & Zervas, C.E. (2012). Modelling sea-level rise impacts on storm surges along U.S. coasts. Environmental Research Letters, 7; IOP Publishing.

Totty, M. (2011). How to build a greener city. *The Wall Street Journal*, September 12, 2011.

www.ingramcontent.com/pod-product-compliance
Lightning Source LLC
Chambersburg PA
CBHW050120280326
41933CB00010B/1175